Sew To Swap

Quilting Projects to Exchange Online and by Mail

Chrissie Grace

KRAUSE PUBLICATIONS
CINCINNATI, OHIO

Table of Contents

Quilting may conjure up many different images for people. Many people associate quilts with scrap quilts made by women during the Great Depression. Another popular image is of grandmothers sitting together, hand quilting a gift during a weekly quilter's bee. I've always been drawn to the art of quilting, but when I discovered a group of modern quilters a few years ago, I was pulled into a whole new world that breaks many quilting stereotypes.

Modern quilting is a fresh approach to the traditional art of quilting. Modern quilters take traditional quilt blocks and update them in fresh and current ways. We also use modern fabrics, change up block arrangements and create our own quilt blocks. Many traditional quilt blocks have been modified by modern quilters, giving them a "wonky," or skewed, look.

The word *quilting* refers to the stitches that hold the layers of a quilt together; modern quilters have a new view on this, as well. Straight-line quilting is popular for a clean look. Stippling and loopy quilting, or free motion quilting, have become popular techniques as well. While modern quilts reflect trends and current aesthetics, they also highlight the quilter's personal style.

In October 2009 the founding branch of The Modern Quilt Guild began in Los Angeles. As of today, there are over 90 branches worldwide, and the groups are growing. Joining The Modern Quilt Guild, or any local guild, can provide you with support and education. In addition to things like workshops, field trips, charity quilts and show-'n-tells, modern guilds often host fabric swaps and block swaps. Swapping is a very fun and exciting way to quilt.

I started participating in virtual swaps about a year ago and became hooked. While the projects in this book are geared for any kind of swapping group, I "met" these contributors online via blogs and swap groups. This book will give you a lot of information on virtual swapping, but please keep in mind that the swaps can be modified to fit a local swapping group as well.

Fabric swaps are perfect for beginning quilters who aren't quite sure if their construction skills are ready to share with others. They are also a great way to collect a variety of fabrics. We tend to buy the same types of fabric for ourselves. Fabric swapping puts new fabrics into your collection, particularly pieces that you may not have purchased. Allowing someone else's taste to influence your fabric choices can help broaden your fabric collection, which in turn can add variety and interest to your quilt-making.

The spectrum of quilt block swapping is so large that I don't even know where to begin. The possibilities are limitless. You can swap with just one person and give each other a theme, such as a type of project, material specifications or a color scheme. You can swap small quilted projects or individual blocks. There are swaps for using leftover fabrics, swaps based on holidays, virtual quilting bees, quilt-alongs, swaps for charities, swaps for improv blocks and swaps based on colors or a trendy theme. The possibilities are endless, and once you get started, it will be hard to stop.

This book was written for those of you who are interested in becoming a quilt swapper. I hope you are inspired by the efforts of the participating quilters. The sheer talent, artistry and work contained in these quilts is overwhelming. The men and women who contributed to the swaps are all amazing quilters. Thank you to my quilting friends and fellow swappers who have taught me so much about the quilting world.

Enjoy the book!

A team of fabulous contributors helped make this book what it is. You will see their thoughts, hints and ideas throughout the book, and their handiwork in every project. For more information on these amazing quilters, see pages 137–139.

Chapter One

Get Ready to Swap

If you picked up this book, chances are you are already a quilter or you want to become one. Even if you've never made a quilt, this chapter contains plenty of information to help you begin. It's important when constructing a quilt that you do it properly—it would be such a shame to spend your precious time and money constructing a quilted project only to have it fall apart later. If you are going to swap your handmade items, you want to send items of quality. Imagine how you would feel receiving an item that was put together poorly.

Becoming a quilt swapper takes you into a realm of quilting that will add a new dimension to your favorite hobby. You will create friendships with people who are interested in and support some of the same passions as you. You will be exposed to new projects, new techniques, new fabrics and new people that you would not otherwise have had the chance to experience. Whether you are a beginning, intermediate or advanced quilter, you are sure to learn new methods and techniques from your fellow swappers, and you will teach them new things, too, as you share your own personal style and way of doing things.

The bottom line here is to have fun! Enjoy the process, make some new friends and share what you love to do with others.

All About Swaps

You may be a modern quilter who is wondering, "Why swap?" As you'll soon discover, there are many benefits to becoming part of a quilt exchange.

Perhaps most importantly, you will develop new friendships. When you participate in a swap, you spend your time and creative energies making something special for someone else, and in return they do the same for you. In doing so, you form a camaraderie through the act of creating. Swapping is also very educational. You will learn more about current fabric trends, popular block patterns and trendy quilted home décor than if you were just sewing for yourself. Lastly, you will be filled with constant inspiration. It is just plain fun to receive what I call "quilty mail." Quilt swappers tend to go all out with their swapping packages. Don't be surprised if you get little extras in your packages like a quilted pin cushion or a package of scraps. There is endless eye candy in the swapping world!

Types of Swaps

There are three main types of swaps. They can be categorized as *centralized*, *decentralized* and *quilting bees*. These swaps differ by the methods used to get items from one quilter to another. They are all great ways to swap, but you may prefer one over the other.

Centralized Quilting Swaps

In this type of swap, participating swappers send their completed items (i.e., blocks) back to the leader of the swap. The swap leader sorts the items, repackages them and mails them back out to the participants. A good example of a centralized swap is THE INVISIBLE NINE PATCH SWAP (page 108).

Pros for Centralized Swaps

• You receive all of your items at once.

• If someone doesn't fulfill their swap requirements, you receive your own items back.

• Postage can be inexpensive.

Cons for Centralized Swaps

• You are more apt to receive items that aren't typically your aesthetic.

• Since there is usually a large amount of people involved in these swaps, they aren't usually very personal.

Decentralized Quilting Swaps

In this type of swap, you send completed items directly to each swap member in your group, and in return you receive an item from each of them. Depending on the item(s) being swapped, you may send and receive only one package (as in THE DOLL QUILT SWAP on page 46), or you may send and receive multiple packages (as in THE HEXIE TABLE RUNNER SWAP on page 38).

Pros for Decentralized Swaps

• You receive a larger influx of "quilty mail." It's fun to run out to your mailbox each day to see what has arrived.

• These types of swaps are much more personal. You have the ability to really spend time finding out what the other person loves.

Cons for Decentralized Swaps

• Postage can be higher since you may be sending out multiple packages.

• There is a chance that another swapper may not follow through, which unfortunately may leave you without items.

Quilting Bees

In this type of swap, you join a group of other quilters and commit to making each person in that group a requested block. Everyone takes a turn until the round is complete. A good example of a quilting bee is THE CURVY BLOCK SWAP (page 94); for that swap, I asked all of the swappers to make a block using curved piecing and a specific fabric line.

Pros for Quilting Bees

• Joining a quilting bee is a great way to expand your knowledge about quilting. You will probably be asked to make blocks that you've never made before or to use fabrics out of your comfort zone. This is a great way to become a better quilter.

Cons for Quilting Bees

• After receiving a variety of blocks for a quilt, you may find you lack the time or energy to put all the blocks together to make the quilt top right away.

• It is easy to get carried away and join a large number of bees, and you can find yourself overwhelmed by all of the commitments.

How to Get Involved Locally

Check out your local sewing stores for established groups that may be accepting new members. Also check in your area for quilting guilds or steady sewing groups. Almost every big city now has a Modern Quilt Guild, so that is an excellent way to start. The Modern Quilt Guilds are newly formed and most are actively looking for new members, providing a great way for you to get involved with a group even if you're new to quilting. For more information, visit www.themodernquiltguild.com.

If you join or are already involved with a group or guild that doesn't have a swapping element, you can start one! Talk to the group leaders to find out how they would like you to proceed, and then go for it. Establish a timetable and deadlines, and consider starting with small, direct-swap items like doll quilts. Once everyone sees the great things that are being made, everyone will want to participate.

Collaborating Online

To get involved in online quilting swaps, you will need to find some online groups to join. One great way to connect is to start your own blog or Flickr site. Both of these are free to start and join, and you will discover that having a place to post pictures of your own projects is a great way to start. A lot of quilting swaps now require a Flickr site so you can share pictures of the items you exchange. All you need is a computer and a digital camera.

If you are looking for an online group to join, here are a few places to start:

• http://quilting.about.com

• www.flickr.com (groups: Quilting Bee Blocks, Fresh Modern Quilts, Sew New to Me Virtual Quilting Bee, Wonderfully {Wonky} Improv Quilts & Blocks!!)

A Few Swap Ideas

Items to swap truly are limited only by your imagination. Look to your favorite blogs, magazines and photo pools to find ideas for you and your friends to exchange. Here are a few ideas to get you started.

Blocks

• One person gets all the blocks in one month; everyone in the group has a turn.

• Each person makes multiple, identical blocks, and everyone involved gets one.

• Blocks are sent to one person who pieces the quilt together and then donates it or auctions it off for charity.

Pin Cushions

The swap is between two partners. Oftentimes, these pin cushions feature miniaturized versions of traditional blocks using modern fabric. Functional and fun!

Doll Quilts or Mini Quilts

The swap is between two partners. These are great for using scraps, trying new techniques or quilting methods, and letting your imagination run free. Small quilts are quick projects that can be used to decorate a sewing space.

Hot Pads, Trivets, Place Mats and Coasters

The swap is between two partners. These swaps are great for experimentation because they're primarily functional. It's also nice to have something pretty on your kitchen table.

Pillows

Pillow swaps between two partners are all the rage! Go crazy with appliqué or piecing, but check first with your partner about color preferences to make sure the pillow coordinates with their décor.

Fabric

Fabric swaps are great for a "live" swap with a large group or guild. Simply take what you bring. For example, if you bring four fat quarters, you get four fat quarters to take home. Try swapping:

• Fat quarters

• Bags of fabric scraps

• Yardage based on a color or other theme

Swapping Guidelines

- Always follow the guidelines given for a particular swap. Make sure you have the time and energy to fulfill what the swap leader is asking for. The most important things to consider before committing to a swap are the time frame, fabric requirements and guidelines for accuracy. It's important not to let other people down.

- Swapping is as much (if not more) about developing friendships and having fun as it is about creating "perfect" quilts. Remember that you wiall be swapping with quilters of varying skill levels. I think most swappers try their hardest, but not all the blocks you receive will be perfect. Everyone is on a different learning curve.

- You may be paired with people who live internationally. If shipping is an issue for you, you may request to ship only within your country.

- It helps to start your own blog or photo site (e.g., Flickr). It is important to show off what you've made and received for various swaps. You'll find that you will quickly become part of quilting and swapping communities, and you will want to share what you've created and received with others.

Ask The Contributors

WHAT'S THE BEST THING YOU'VE EVER RECEIVED IN A SWAP?

Allison: My quilting bee partners made me beautiful Drunkard's Path (circle) blocks. I think they were all cursing my name when they first found out they would be piecing curves, but by the end I think everyone at least learned something, and I ended up with a beautiful quilt.

Angela: A fabulous fairy-tale cottage pin cushion.

Chrissie: I recently did a fabric swap and received tons of fabric that I really wanted for my stash.

Corey: I just received an amazing Christmas swap package that included a tree skirt, a table runner, a mug and a Christmas star. It was just above and beyond what I expected.

John: A Cathedral Windows pillow made by Heather Bostic ({House} of A La Mode) featuring some of my favorite Patty Young fabrics—it's prominently displayed in my home.

Melanie: I was part of a pin cushion swap, and my partner couldn't decide on a pin cushion to send me, so she sent me six! They are all adorable and are either in use or displayed around my sewing room.

Nova: I have *loved* all my swap gifts. I have been lucky to have been partnered with some very talented swappers who nailed my taste and style every time, so I really couldn't pick a favorite.

Ryan: I don't know if this qualifies as the "best thing" I've ever received in a swap, but a personal note from another swapper enclosed in a package makes the recipient appreciate the gift even more. A little insight as to what they were thinking while crafting or how they enjoyed making something for you is priceless.

All About Supplies

You will enjoy your quilting experience much more when you have the correct tools. It is worth the investment to take good care of your tools and invest in high quality materials. They will immensely improve your sewing accuracy. Quilting and sewing don't require a large number of supplies and tools, but make sure you have the basics stocked in your craft space so you have everything you might need before starting a big project.

Sewing Machine

You will need a sewing machine in good working order. Anytime you begin a new project, I suggest cleaning out the bobbin with a little brush. Always insert a new needle when you are starting a new project. A dull needle can lead to inaccurate quilting. Refer to the manual that came with your machine for troubleshooting advice and more information on how to operate your particular machine.

Free Motion Foot/Darning Foot

Free motion quilting allows you to create fancy patterns and designs while machine stitching. Using a free motion foot and lowering your machine's feed dogs gives you control over where the fabric moves under the needle. The length of the stitches is controlled by the sewing speed and how fast you move the fabric under the needle. It takes practice to accurately stitch a design with even stitches. Use both hands to guide the fabric under the foot. Rubberized gloves will help you grip the fabric while free motion quilting.

¼" Foot

When piecing, a ¼" seam allowance is standard. Using a ¼" foot makes accurately maintaining this seam allowance much easier. When you sew two pieces of fabric together, keep the edges of the fabric aligned with the edge of the ¼" foot to maintain your seam allowance.

If you can't find a ¼" foot, mark the seam allowance on your machine bed. Place a ruler under your machine's needle and measure ¼" to the right of the needle. Mark this measurement off with painters tape. Align the edges of your fabric with the left-hand edge of the tape to maintain a ¼" seam allowance. Check the accuracy of your mark by sewing two pieces together and then measuring the seam allowance. Adjust the tape as necessary.

Walking Foot

A walking foot is necessary when machine quilting. It is used for all straight-line quilting. A walking foot moves the top layer of fabric under the needle at the same rate as the feed dogs are moving the bottom layer, which prevents the quilt layers from puckering and pleating. You can also use your walking foot for attaching the binding, stitching in the ditch and continuous curve quilting.

Free motion foot, ¼" foot and walking foot (left to right)

Use a free motion foot and rubberized gloves for controlled free motion quilting.

Mark a ¼" seam allowance on the machine bed with painter's tape.

Scissors

You should have a pair of fabric scissors that are used exclusively for cutting fabric; cutting paper will dull the scissor blades. You also need a pair of small scissors or snips to clip threads when sewing.

Rotary Cutters

Be extremely careful when using a rotary cutter. It has a round razor blade and can cause deep cuts. When it's not in use, always place the protective guard over the blade. When your rotary cutter is not cutting easily anymore, it's time to replace the blade. There are many styles of cutters available. I suggest one with a 2½" blade—it can cut through multiple layers and is comfortable to hold.

Rotary Cutting Mat

A cutting mat is used with a rotary cutter to protect the work surface and the rotary cutter blade. I recommend purchasing the largest mat you can. A good size for most quilting work is 18" x 24". Cutting mats are marked in a 1" grid on one side and are blank on the other. Mats should be placed on a firm surface and stored flat. Take care to keep mats away from heat because they will warp.

Acrylic Ruler

Acrylic see-through rulers are used to align the fabric and hold it firmly against the mat while cutting. There are a large variety of sizes available, but if you only have one, be sure it is a 6" x 24" rotary ruler, which can make nearly any type of cut. It should be marked with 30-, 45- and 60-degree lines, with dimensions in ⅛" increments.

Threads

A large selection of thread is available to today's quilter. For best results, always use a high quality thread that matches the project. My personal preference when quilting with cottons is a 50/3 medium-weight 100% cotton thread.

Pins

You'll need long straight pins to hold fabric pieces together while sewing. Choose very thin needles with large heads.

Batting

There are a lot of batting choices on the market. Each has its own positives and negatives. There are polyester, cotton and a cotton/poly blend. Polyester is warmer than cotton, is durable enough to withstand a lot of washings and gives a "puffier" look to your quilt. Cotton usually shrinks slightly but can be prewashed. Cotton is lightweight and durable and is easier to quilt than polyester. The cotton/poly blend is generally considered to provide the best features of both polyester and cotton battings.

Seam Ripper

In case of mistakes—and there will be some!—always keep your seam ripper handy.

Needles

There are three basic needle types: sharp, ballpoint and universal. Sharps are used for sewing dense fabrics and for topstitching. Ballpoints are used for sewing knits. A universal needle has a tapered point and a slightly stronger shaft for stitching through multiple layers, making it ideal for quilting.

Iron and Ironing Board

Any iron and ironing board you already have will work just fine. If you don't own an iron, find one that's fairly heavy because it's the combination of weight and heat that presses your quilting components. I like an iron with nice steam control, although some people prefer to use a spray bottle with water.

Basting Spray

Spray basting has become my favorite way of basting. It is easy, fast and accurate. It saves your fingers from pins, and there are no pinholes in your fabric to deal with later. Use basting spray with caution—always make sure there is adequate ventilation because the fumes are toxic.

All About Fabric

One of my favorite things about quilting is shopping for new fabrics—I think most quilters would agree with that statement! So much beautiful fabric is available, and with so many local and online fabric shops, it is all so accessible. New fabric lines come out on a regular basis, so there is something new to choose from almost all the time. Building your fabric stash is something that takes time, but eventually you will own a nice selection of fabrics in every color of the rainbow. Be careful to store your fabric stash out of direct sunlight because the sun can fade your fabrics over time.

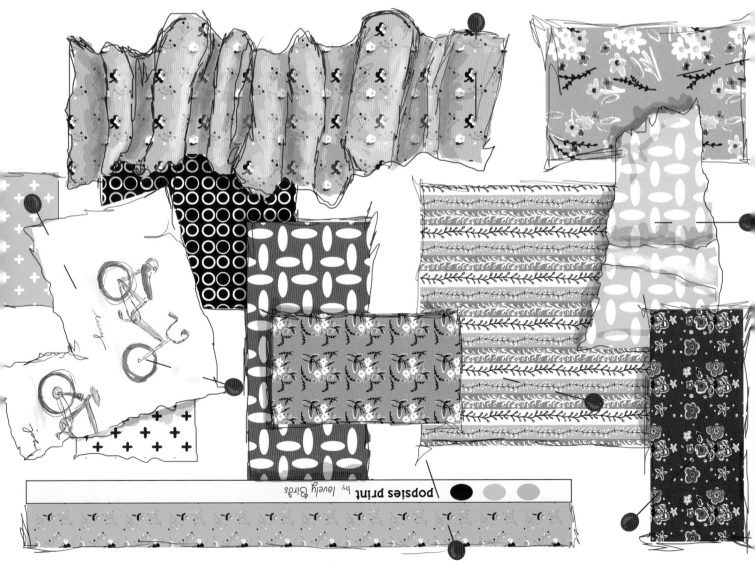

popsies print by lovely birds

The Best Part . . . Fabric!

One way you can immediately tell a modern quilter from a traditional quilter is by his or her fabric choices. Most modern guilds and swap groups have a list of fabrics that many modern quilters have in their stash. When participating in swaps, be sure to keep up with the latest trends. Some current modern trends include:

• Minimalist approach using a lot of solid colors

• Geometric prints and patterns

• The use of bright colors with a dark gray background

• Mixing fabric lines with a white background

• Color combos such as pink/aqua/red, gray/yellow and turquoise/orange

• The use of different fabric blends such as double gauze and linen

• White fabrics with splashes of bright colors

• Neutral palettes with a lot of quilting texture

100% Quilting Cotton and Beyond

When choosing fabrics for your quilts, it is best to use 100% quilting cottons. Cottons are the most common fabrics for quilting because they are easy to sew, strong and usually colorfast. (Colorfast fabrics contain dyes that are resistant to fading or running.) Cotton fabrics are excellent at maintaining their shape and color, which is really important when making a quilt that you would like to use for a long time. Most of the fabrics you see online and in quilting stores are 100% cotton, but it's always good to double check on the end of the bolt.

Flannel is another popular quilting fabric. It adds a little weight, has a very soft texture and adds a great deal of warmth. Linen is also a popular choice among modern quilters. It is especially nice when juxtaposed with bright colors. Be careful with linen though—it has a loose weave that is prone to ravel.

Be aware: knits, crepes and stretch materials are very difficult to sew with, so avoid using these materials when quilting.

When it is time to purchase backing material for your quilts, it is wise to use one that is a similar weight and color as the top of your quilt. Using the same types of materials for the top and bottom makes the whole quilt easier to sew through.

WHEN YOU NEED A QUILTING BREAK, WHAT'S YOUR FAVORITE SNACK?

Allison: Anything! I've got a bad habit of taking a snack break in between sewing each row of a quilt. Lately I much on raw almonds—at least they're healthy.

Angela: Chocolate!

Chrissie: Spicy Cheetos, but I have to make sure to wash my hands so I don't get orange fingerprints on the quilt.

Corey: More often than not I get something to drink. Sweet tea is a current fave.

Crystal: Peanut butter M&Ms.

John: I don't usually snack while quilting, although I'll never turn down a homemade chocolate chip cookie.

Melanie: I don't snack when I sew. I like to keep my hands and workspace free of any potential messes.

Nettie: I *never* eat while I am quilting because I don't like to have dirty hands.

Nova: I'm a savory girl and anything cheesy always hits the spot.

Ryan: I always keep a snack handy for small bursts of energy in the middle of a marathon quilting session! Some of my staples are mini pretzels, goldfish crackers and small chocolate bars.

Tips on Buying Fabric

When you are buying fabric, it is better to be safe than sorry. Always buy a little more than you need; that way if you mess up or need more, it's there. You can always find another place to use your leftover fabrics and scraps, but if you run out, you may find yourself unable to replace the fabric, which could ruin your whole quilt.

There are many ways to buy fabric, and patterns will often dictate your choice. Here are the most common ways to buy your quilting fabrics:

- **Bolt**: Buying fabric straight from the bolt can be cost-effective in many cases. If you are an avid quilter and know you will be using that particular fabric often, it is best to buy off the bolt. Each bolt varies anywhere from 8 yards to 25 yards. You can buy the entire bolt or an amount in yardage cut from the bolt.

- **Jelly rolls**: A jelly roll is a roll of strips of fabric. Each strip is 2½" wide and the length is determined by the width of the fabric (anywhere from 40"–45").

- **Honey buns**: A honey bun is a roll of strips of fabric. Each strip is 1½" wide and the length is determined by the width of the fabric (anywhere from 40"–45"). They are available in some fabric collections and are especially helpful for the tiniest cuts in quilting.

- **Charm packs**: A charm pack is a stack of fabric squares that are precut to measure 5" x 5". Charm packs are available by collection and typically include forty-two pieces of fabric.

- **Layer cakes**: A layer cake is a stack of fabric squares that are precut to measure 10" x 10". They are similar to a charm pack but at a larger size. Layer cakes are available by collection and typically include forty-two pieces of fabric.

- **Fat quarters**: A fat quarter is ¼-yard cut of fabric that is cut wide, not long. A fat quarter's approximate size is 18" x 22". Fat quarters are a very popular way to buy fabric and a great way to build your stash.

Info on Fabric Grain

I know from personal experience that it can be confusing for a beginning quilter when people start talking about the *grain of a fabric*. It is wise for you to learn about fabric grain because it will affect how your pieces are cut and how stable the fabric is after cutting.

Fabric grain refers to the way threads are arranged in a piece of fabric. With cotton and linen fabrics, the grain is perpendicular and parallel to the selvages. When you cut your fabric along the grain, it will remain stable and good for piecing.

In quilting terms, we refer to any cut that doesn't run along a straight grain as a bias cut. Fabric that has been cut on the bias is more apt to stretch along the edges and needs to be handled more carefully. For example, triangles always have at least one bias edge. The best placement for a bias edge is usually on a block's interior, not on an outside edge. For optimal stabilization, sew the bias edge to a straight-of-grain edge whenever possible.

To test your's fabric grain, cut a small square of cotton fabric with the edges parallel to the straight grains. Tug on the fabric square from side to side in both directions. You should see and feel a difference. The lengthwise grain has less stretch. Tug on the fabric square from one corner to the other—the bias. It should stretch a lot. If you pull too hard, you will see that the fabric is permanently altered. Understanding fabric grain will making sewing your quilts a lot easier.

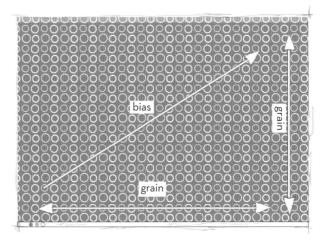

Understanding fabric grain

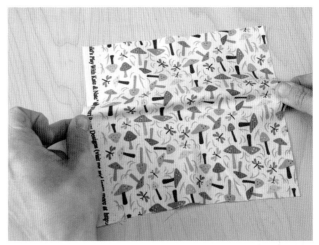

Pull from side to side (straight grain).

Pull on the diagonal (bias).

Choosing Colors

Most fabrics are available as a collection, so you can easily find a color scheme that is appealing to you and then purchase the whole collection. However, it can be much more fun and original to create a mix of fabrics yourself. When pairing your own fabrics, it helps to have a good grasp on color theory.

Owning a color wheel is a great tool for any quilter. The color wheel can help you understand the relationship between colors, making fabric selection a lot easier.

Reds, oranges and yellows are warm colors that tend to pop. Greens, blues and violets are cool colors that tend to recede.

There are three main types of color combinations:

- **Complementary colors**: Complementary colors are *opposite* colors, meaning they are across from each other on the color wheel. When combined, they create a lot of visual contrast. An example of a complementary color scheme would be the trendy combination of orange and aqua.

- **Monochromatic colors**: A monochromatic quilt is made up of only one color. For example, combining fabrics that are all red but have different patterns, values and shades would produce a monochromatic quilt.

- **Analogous colors**: To select fabrics for an analogous color scheme, pick colors that are next to each other on the color wheel. For example, you could make a cool quilt with greens, blues and purples, or a warm quilt with reds, oranges and yellows.

Modern quilters often pair black and/or white fabrics with different colors to provide strong contrast. For example, they are often used for sashing. The same is true for other neutral colors, such as grays and browns. Gray solids are particulary popular right now, as are the soft browns found in linens. It is a good idea to have variations of solid black, white and other neutral fabrics in your stash because they can add a lot of interest to your designs.

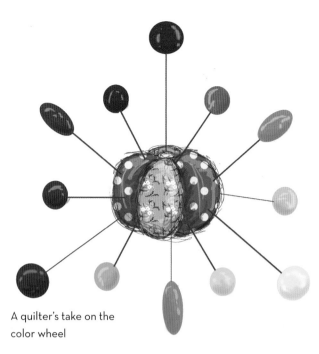

A quilter's take on the color wheel

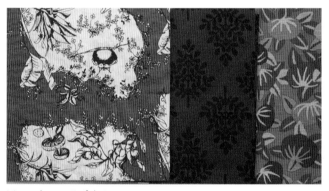

Complementary fabrics

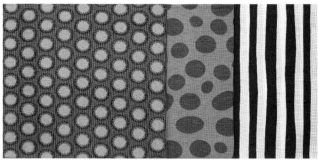

Monochromatic fabrics

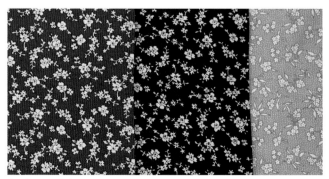

Analogous fabrics

Prewashing Fabrics

There is a small debate among quilters as to whether it is advisable to prewash your fabric before quilting. Most quilters I know do not prewash their fabrics, but there are many others who do. There are pros and cons for both sides.

Some People Prewash . . .

Some cotton fabrics bleed, especially vivid colors like red and purple. Some people don't want to take the chance of those colors bleeding through onto a finished quilt. Another reason to prewash is that some cotton fabrics may shrink more than others. Uneven shrinkage could cause puckers and distortions the first time the quilt is washed. Lastly, some people prefer to remove chemicals and odors that new fabrics can retain from the factory.

. . . And Some People Don't

First of all, some people are so excited to work with their new fabric that they don't want to take the time to wash and press it. Washing your fabric can also make it feel limp, and some people don't like that. A lot of modern quilters like the crinkly look you get after washing a finished quilt when you don't prewash your fabrics, and they don't want to lose that.

I personally choose not to prewash my fabrics, but when I use strong fabric colors like red, I wash the quilt with a color-absorbing pad, available at most quilting or craft stores.

Ask The Contributors

HOW DO YOU GET INSPIRED WHEN YOU'RE FEELING A LACK OF CREATIVITY?

Allison: I start sewing my random scraps together. I might not be in the mood to begin with, but usually this sparks my creativity and is a good stress reliever at the same time.

Chrissie: I go through my quilting books for a pattern I'd like to try, or I get online and browse through Flickr.

Corey: I am inspired by so many different things—sometimes fabric inspires a quilt, a quilt block just begs to be made, or I will see something that someone else has made and I'll take it in a different direction.

Crystal: I try to get other things done—laundry, cleaning, etc. Too much of *that* gets me back to the sewing machine in no time.

John: That's easy—I jump on Flickr and browse the various modern quilting and swap sites. They never fail to deliver gobs and gobs of inspiration.

Melanie: A trip to the bookstore or library is usually in order when I'm feeling uncreative.

Nettie: I am inspired from everything around me. I spend most of my days with my kids and like to think that most of my inspiration comes from them—their toys, colors in their clothes, patterns at the park . . . I love bright and subdued. I am also *very* inspired by the many quilting/crafting blogs and online sites.

Ryan: A favorite way to clear my head when I'm in a creative funk is to surf the Internet on photo-sharing sites like Flickr and to read blogs. There are millions of other creative people out there who are willing to talk about and share pictures of their projects. A good conversation with another artist is all I need to get my imagination going again.

All About Quilting

The durability and beauty of your quilts begin with knowledge and preparation. As with many things in life, there is more than one correct way to make a quilt. This section describes the tried-and-true methods that I have learned along the way. You may figure out different ways to do things as you develop your own personal style of quilting. Just remember, safety first.

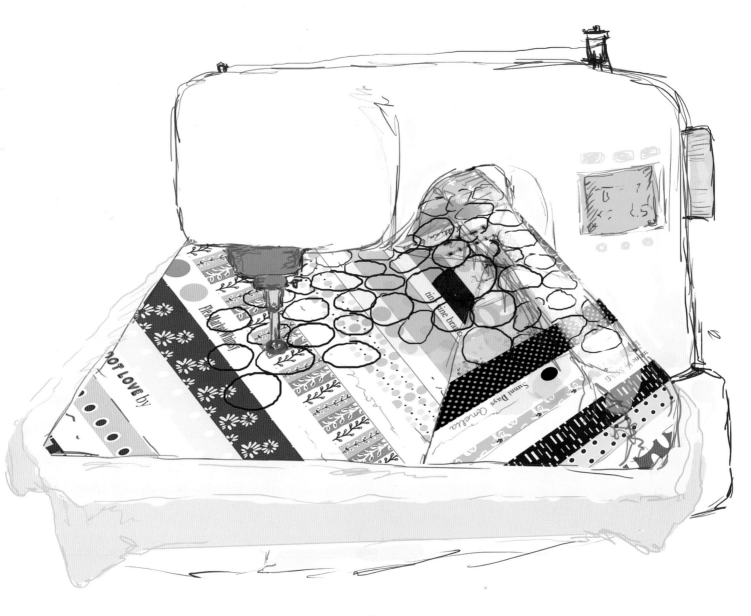

Pressing

Whether you prewash your fabrics or not (page 21), you should always press your fabric before cutting it. It is very important that your fabric is wrinkle-free for accurate cutting.

It is also important that you press your seams. Depending on the project, you will sometimes press all your seams open, and other times in one direction. Unless a project includes directions for pressing, you will need to find which you prefer. I prefer to press my seams open. After years of pressing them one way or the other, I tried pressing them open and found I got a more even block. When pressing seams, it helps to first run your finger along the seams, gently finger pressing them with a firm but smooth motion.

Pressing the seam allowance to the side

Pressing the seam allowance open

Rotary Cutting Basics

One of the most important steps to achieving accurate cutting results is changing your rotary blade on a regular basis. Before you start any new project, make sure your blade is still sharp. As you cut, the blade should slice through the fabric like butter. If you have to cut the fabric twice, you need to change the blade. Remember to be very careful with new blades! They are extremely sharp and can cause very serious cuts. Always close the safety cover over the rotary cutter blade when it's not in use.

To Cut Fabric:

1 Fold the fabric in half, matching the selvages at the top. The folded edge should be closest to you. Place the fabric on the cutting mat, keeping the selvages even. Smooth out any wrinkles.

2 Place a 6" × 24" ruler on top of the fabric on the right-hand side. Line up your ruler so that a horizontal line on the ruler matches up to the fold. Line up the right side of the ruler.

3 Cut off a small strip of the fabric by holding the rotary cutter against the right edge of the ruler and rolling it away from you using firm, downward pressure. As you slowly cut through the fabric, walk your fingers up the ruler. This makes it less likely that your ruler will move. Creating this straight edge is called "squaring up the fabric." The right-hand edge of your fabric should now be perfectly perpendicular to the bottom fold.

4 Without moving the fabric, move to the other side of your cutting mat. To cut strips, determine the width of the strips needed. Align the correct measurement on the ruler with the straightened fabric edge. Cut along the side of the ruler. Continue to make cuts until you have cut the number of strips needed for your quilt.

Fold the fabric in half, matching the selvages.

Square up the fabric edge.

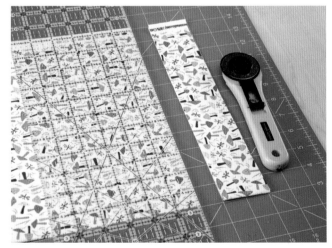

Cut strips from the fabric.

Piecing

Remember to check the stitching and tension on your sewing machine before you begin. All sewing machines are different, but most people set their machines to about twelve stitches per inch when piecing. When starting a new project, I always change out my needle. Needles can be very persnickety and can significantly affect the quality of your stitches. I also like to make sure that my bobbin is fully wound and is inserted properly. There is nothing more frustrating than trying to sew a quilt top and losing time to deal with machine issues.

Piecing can be described as the act of sewing together all the separate pieces of a quilt top. Machine-piecing requires very precise seams. A $\frac{1}{4}$" seam allowance is standard in quilting. If your machine does not come with a $\frac{1}{4}$" sewing machine foot, I suggest that you invest in one for more accurate seams (page 13).

If you are a very relaxed quilter or you are making a "wonky" block, accuracy isn't quite as important. On the other hand, if you'd like your piecing to be closer to perfection, cut your fabrics accurately, be careful with your seam allowances and press your seams consistently.

I suggest practicing with scrap materials before you begin working on a quilt. Perfect piecing comes more naturally to some people than others. I am not one that it comes easily to, so I have to be very careful with my steps.

Use $\frac{1}{4}$" feet to maintain an accurate seam allowance.

A perfectly pieced Nine Patch block

A wonky Nine Patch block

Adding Borders

Sometimes you may think you're finished with a quilt, but it just needs that . . . *something*. Some people are intimidated by adding borders because they can turn out slightly crooked or wavy, but adding borders to a quilt top can often take it from good to great. Here is a surefire way to get straight and even borders.

To Add Borders:

1 Lay your well-pressed quilt top on a clean, flat surface. Measure the width of the quilt three times with a tape measure: once across the top, once across the middle and once across the bottom. (If the three measurements are the same, you are amazing—mine are never perfect!)

2 Find the average of the three measurements by adding them together and then dividing by 3. Round to the nearest whole number. This measurement is the length you will need to cut for the top and bottom borders.

For example:
- *$29\frac{3}{4}" + 30\frac{1}{2}" + 29\frac{1}{4}" = 89\frac{1}{2}"$*
- *$89\frac{1}{2}" \div 3 = 29.8333"$ (round up to 30")*

3 The border width is up to you, depending on how you want your finished quilt to look. Just remember, when you cut the border strips, add $\frac{1}{2}"$ to the width to allow for the seam allowance. Cut two border strips to the desired width and the length you figured out in step 2.

For example: If you want a finished border width of 3", cut your borders $3\frac{1}{2}"$ wide.

4 Fold each border strip in half lengthwise and mark the middle with a pin. Fold it again in quarters and mark the quarter points with pins. Do this with the top and bottom edges of the quilt top as well, marking the half and quarter points with pins.

Measure the width of the quilt three times with a tape measure.

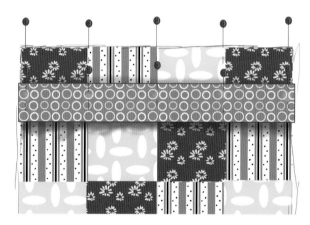

Mark the half and quarter points of the border strip and quilt with pins.

5 To ensure that the border does not get stretched as you sew, pin the top border piece to the top edge of the quilt top, right sides together, matching up the pins. Sew the fabric together with a standard $1/4$" seam. Repeat with the bottom border. Press both borders open.

6 Again, measure the quilt three times, this time from top to bottom through the middle and on both sides. Be sure to include the borders in these measurements. Find the average of the three numbers, just like you did in step 2. This is the length you will need to cut the side borders.

7 Repeat the same process to cut, mark, pin and attach the side borders. You can add multiple borders to your quilt by repeating these instructions.

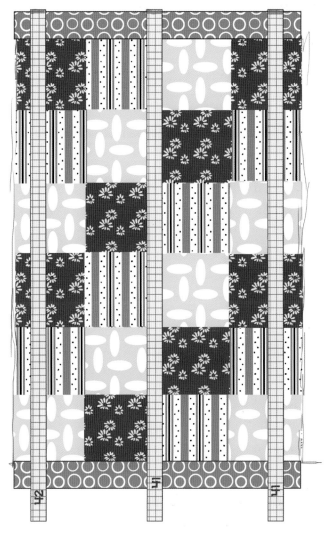

Measure the height of the quilt three times with a tape measure.

Finish by sewing the side borders to the quilt.

Piecing a Back

The back of a quilt is traditionally made of one coordinating fabric that complements the quilt top, but many modern quilters piece the backs of their quilts. If you are making a pieced back that is larger than a lap quilt, you will probably need two lengths of fabric to make the back wide enough. (Fabric usually comes in a standard 44" width.)

Although it is easier and not as time-consuming to use one piece of fabric for the back, piecing the back usually makes for a much more interesting overall quilt design. It is also a great opportunity to use the fabric scraps left over from the front of your quilt. It is definitely worth the time!

There are quite a few ways to piece your backing. Here are a couple of great ideas:

• Cut large strips from the main quilt fabrics and sash them with a solid fabric. The strips could run horizontally or vertically across your backing.

• Make a few extra blocks that you based the quilt top on, and piece them together to create a break in the back. For example, if you made a log cabin quilt, make a few extra log cabin blocks to use on the back.

Here are a few tips to remember when creating the quilt backing:

• Some fabric manufacturers offer wide yardage for backings (approximately 110").

• Remember to trim the selvage edge off your fabric. Leaving the selvage on your quilt backing can cause it to pucker during quilting.

• The backing fabric (as well as the batting) needs to be larger than the quilt top. Most quilters agree that it's best to have at least 2" of extra batting and backing extending past each side of the quilt top. That means your backing and batting should be at least 4" wider and 4" longer than your quilt top.

• If you are a beginning quilter, a backing with a busy print can hide quilting stitches that aren't perfect.

Note: The dimensions for the quilt backs are included in each pattern.

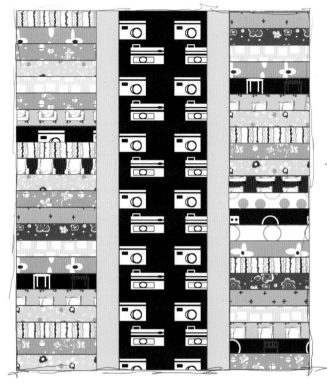

Strips sashed with solids on the quilt back

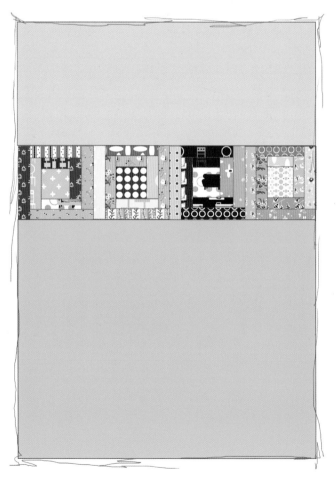

Log cabins create a break in the quilt back.

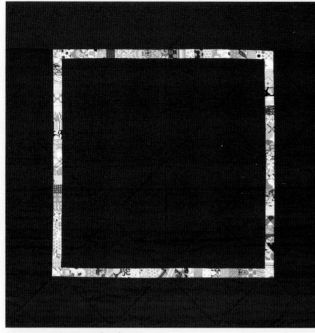

SCRAPBUSTER QUILT back

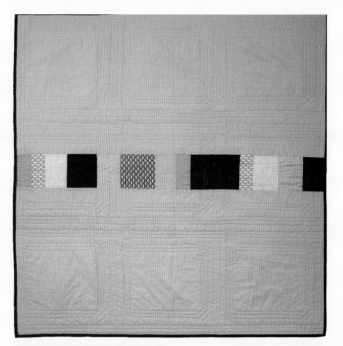

INVISIBLE NINE PATCH QUILT back

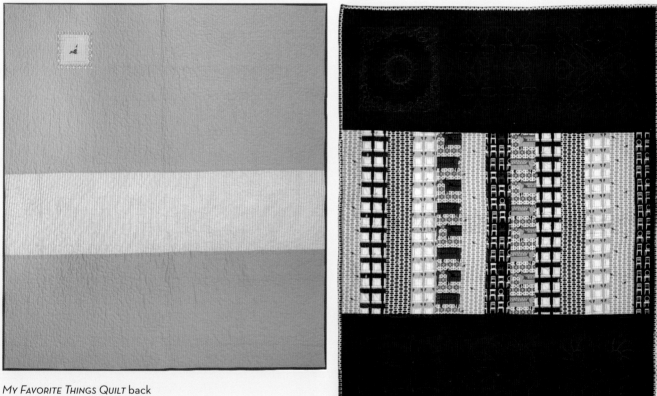

MY FAVORITE THINGS QUILT back

CURVY QUILT back

Making a Quilt Sandwich

When you have completed the quilt top and backing, it is time to assemble the three layers of your quilt. This is also known as making your quilt sandwich.

Make sure the top and backing are pressed well. Find a clean, flat surface that is large enough to lay the quilt back right-side-down. Smooth it very carefully, starting in the center and smoothing toward the edges. Use masking tape to tape down the edges. The fabric should be wrinkle-free and taut, but be careful not to stretch it or pull too tight. Avoid taping down the corners—this can cause the bias to stretch.

Now place the batting on top of the backing and smooth it out in the same way. Finally, place the quilt top right-side-up on top of the batting and smooth it out. Check to make sure that the batting and backing are even on all sides underneath the quilt top.

Layer the backing, batting and quilt top to make a quilt sandwich.

Basting

Allison from the blog Cluck, Cluck Sew will be the first quilter to tell you that "basting is the most important step in making your quilt because if it's not done correctly, it can ruin your quilt, no matter how good of a quilter you are!" She advises to "take the time to make it as perfect as you can." I agree with her wholeheartedly. You've already put a lot of time, energy, money and resources into your quilt. You want this part to go smoothly.

There are three ways to baste a quilt: You can use basting stitches, a temporary basting spray or basting pins. Most quilters use the pin-basting method.

To pin-baste, you will use quilting pins. They look very similar to safety pins, but they have a curve along one side. This curve allows them to go through all three layers of your quilt without causing bunching. Start in the center of your quilt top and work toward the edges, pinning every 4"–6" through all three layers of the quilt. When you have finished pinning, check the back of your quilt to make sure that you didn't accidently crumple the backing fabric during the pinning. If you did, unpin, smooth and re-pin.

Note: Remember to remove the pins as you quilt each area. If you inadvertently sew over the pins, it can break your sewing machine needle.

Using curved quilting pins to baste

Using adhesive basting spray to baste

30

Choosing Thread

Before you begin quilting, you will need to decide what color thread to use for the top and in the bobbin. If you'd like to really show off your quilting, use thread in a contrasting color. For example, if your quilt has a lot of white and light colors in it, use a dark thread for high contrast. If you'd like your quilting to be more subtle, use a matching color with low contrast.

Quilting Techniques

Actually quilting your quilt will probably either be your favorite part of the process or the part that intimidates you the most. There are a lot of qualified long-arm quilters who will do the quilting for a moderate price. Some people prefer to pass their quilt over at this point for fear of "messing it up," while others feel like they aren't "real" quilters unless they follow the process all the way through. I don't consider myself a professional quilter, so depending on the quilt top and size, I may either quilt it myself or hire someone to do it for me. Do whatever feels comfortable for you. Either way, you should at some point try quilting your project yourself. There are two ways to quilt: hand quilting and machine quilting.

Hand Quilting

Hand quilting is the most traditional way to finish a quilt. You need a quilting hoop, a thimble and some special needles (called *betweens*). Hand quilting is achieved by sewing straight, running stitches through all three layers (see photo on page 6). It is very slow, but some people enjoy the quiet, thoughtful process. If your project is small enough, hand quilting provides a portable project that you can take on a long car trip.

Ask The Contributors

DO YOU LIKE TO SEE THE QUILTING STITCHES ON THE BACK OF YOUR QUILT, OR DO YOU PREFER THEM TO BLEND?

Allison: I prefer using a patterned, light-colored backing fabric so my stitches blend in.

Angela: I like the look of quilting's texture, but I try to choose a thread color that will blend in with the backing.

Chrissie: I think that the quilting is as much an expression of creativity as the pattern and fabric selections, so I love for it to be on display.

Corey: I don't really mind either way—I don't care for a lot of contrast between my thread color and backing fabric, though.

Crystal: Yes, I love the texture.

John: Yes, I think the back is just as important as the front.

Kelly: It depends: If I'm using an allover design (like a meander), I like for it to show on the back. If I'm doing something more specific to the particular quilt pattern, I like for it to blend in on the back because the quilting design alone might look strange.

Melanie: I've recently developed a love for hand quilting, and I really like it when it shows on the back. My latest hand quilting project was done in nearly forty different colors of perle cotton, and I love the back as much as the front.

Nova: Oh yes, I love quilting stitches to show on the back. For me, the backs of quilts need to be as interesting as the fronts, even if they're very simple.

Ryan: I think the back of the quilt can sometimes be just as interesting as the front.

Machine Quilting

You don't need a large, expensive long-arm machine to machine quilt. Using a regular sewing machine, you can quilt using two basic techniques: free motion quilting and straight-line quilting. Depending on the quilt top, both of these techniques are used frequently by modern quilters.

To begin, you need a large worktable that will accommodate your machine and quilt. Roll up one side of the quilt so it fits under the machine. Unroll and reroll the quilt as you quilt one small area at a time. It helps to keep a magnetic pin holder nearby so you can remove your pins and have a convenient spot to keep them. Some people like to start in one corner of the quilt and work their way back and forth across the width. I prefer to start in the center and work my way out to avoid puckers. If your quilt is properly basted, it really shouldn't matter.

When you begin quilting, manually bring the sewing machine needle down and back up again. Pull the bobbin thread through your quilt sandwich and put the presser foot down. To create a knot, make several stitches in place. If you need to stop and start while quilting, repeat this method each time.

Free Motion Quilting

I prefer free motion quilting because it is like drawing with your machine needle. It allows you to be creative and is more free-form. However, before you begin on your quilt, I suggest practicing with scrap fabric and batting. Set up your machine by lowering the feed dogs and setting the stitch length to zero (check your machine's manual if you need help doing this). You will also need to use a free motion quilting foot or a darning foot.

Tips when free motion quilting:

- Check the back of your quilt on a regular basis when quilting. Sometimes the top looks fine, but if there is a tension problem, it could affect the back.

- Invest in a pair of quilting gloves. They help tremendously in keeping the quilt flat and in moving the quilt around without slipping.

- Free motion quilting uses a lot of thread, so it helps to have extra bobbins wound and ready to go.

Try free motion quilting to create lots of designs.

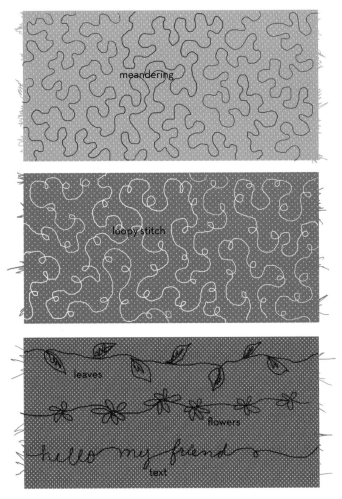

Some common free motion quilting designs

Straight-Line Quilting

A lot of modern quilters love straight-line quilting because it has a clean, simplistic look that often goes well with modern fabrics. With straight-line quilting, you need to use a walking foot with your machine. I suggest using fabric scraps and batting to practice before starting on your quilt. You also need blue painters tape.

Place the edge of one piece of tape where you want your first line, and remove the basting pins under it. Some people measure where they want their lines, and some just eyeball it. Once you have the tape where you want it, position the edge of the walking foot even with the edge of the tape. Sew down the edge of the tape, keeping the edge of the foot aligned with the edge of the tape. After sewing down the full length of the tape, pull up the tape and reposition it for the next line. Continue doing this until your tape loses its stickiness, and then start with a fresh piece.

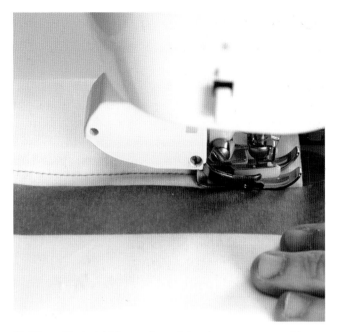

Quilting with straight lines using painters tape as a seam guide.

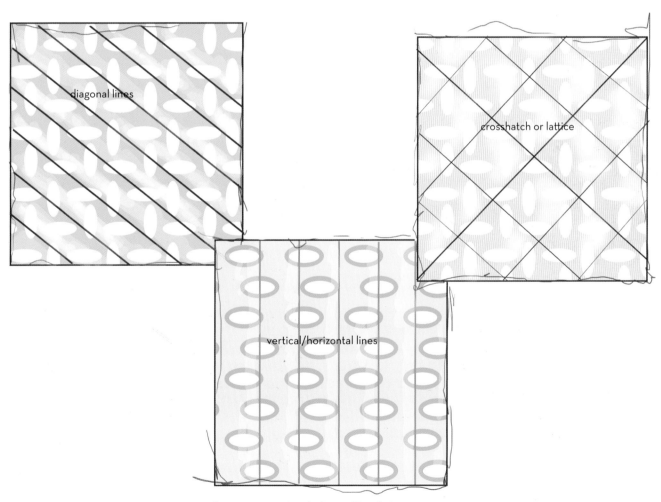

diagonal lines

crosshatch or lattice

vertical/horizontal lines

Some common straight-line quilting designs

Binding

After you have completed the quilting, the final step is to finish off the raw edges by binding the quilt. Binding can be intimidating, but if you take your time and complete each step properly, you will be very proud of the end results. You can either hand sew or machine stitch your binding. Most quilters agree that completing the binding by hand is preferable, so that is the method I will show you.

To Bind:

1 Prepare your quilt by trimming all the way around the quilt top using your long ruler. Align a straight line on your ruler with the raw edges of the quilt top and cut the excess batting and backing even with the edges of the top.

2 Determine the number of binding strips you need for your entire quilt. First, measure the full perimeter of your quilt in inches. Add 12" to this number (it's always better to make a little extra than not have enough at the end) and divide by 40" (or the width of your fabric from selvage to selvage). Round this number up to the nearest whole number to determine the number of binding strips you need.

For example:

• *100" quilt perimeter + 12" = 112"*

• *112" ÷ 40" = 2.8 (rounded up to 3)*

• *You will need 3 binding strips for a 100" quilt.*

3 Cut the determined number of binding strips by cutting strips of material between 2" and 2$^1/_2$" wide. Cut the binding on the lengthwise grain of the fabric (parallel to the selvage) because the fabric is more stable in this direction.

4 Sew all the binding strips together using a 45-degree seam. Trim off the excess corner and iron the binding in half lengthwise, wrong sides together.

5 Beginning at the bottom middle of the front of the quilt, place the raw edges of the binding even with the raw edge of the quilt top. Leave about 6" of extra binding unsewn when you begin. Using a walking foot and a $^1/_4$" seam allowance, start sewing the binding onto the quilt.

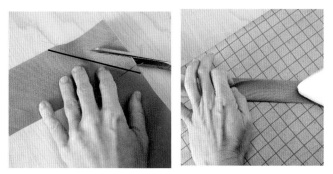

Join strips with a 45-degree seam, trim the seam allowance and press the strip in half.

Sew the raw edges of the binding even with the raw edge of the quilt top.

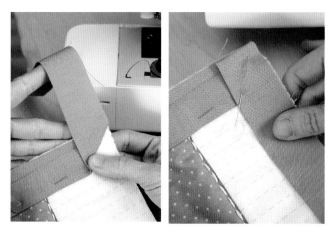

When you reach the corner, flip the binding up and then down, even with the quilt edge.

6 Before you reach a corner, place a pin ¼" away from the bottom edge. Sew until you reach the pin. With the needle down, turn the quilt 45 degrees clockwise and sew to the edge. Turn the quilt toward you, flip the binding up and then down, even with the quilt edge.

7 Begin sewing ¼" from the corner edge and continue sewing around the perimeter of the quilt until you're about 12" from your starting point. You should have a 6" unsewn binding "tail" at the beginning and end of your binding.

8 Fold back the binding tails until the folds meet. Use a water-soluble fabric marker to draw this folded line on the right and wrong side of both tails. Align the drawn line on the right side of the tails, and sew along the line to join the strips. Trim off the excess seam allowance, and finish sewing the binding to the front of the quilt.

9 Wrap the binding around to the back of the quilt. Using a hand sewing needle and matching thread, sew the binding down to the back. Blindstitch along the edges every ⅛"–¼". When you reach a corner, pin and fold the edges in until you have a mitered corner, and sew in place. Snap-in-place hair clips are great to help hold the binding in place as you stitch. When you reach the end of the thread, knot it underneath the binding to hide it, and then start with new thread.

Fold back the binding tails until the folds meet.

Align the drawn line on the right side of the tails and sew along the line.

Using a hand sewing needle and matching thread, sew the binding down to the back.

Finishing the Quilt

Adding a label is your last chance to personalize your quilt. I think labels are important whether you are keeping the quilt for yourself or are swapping or gifting it. The label should have your name, your city and the approximate date (i.e., Summer 2011). Fuse or sew it in place.

There are a few ways you can create a label:

• Cross-stitch or hand embroider one.

• If your sewing machine has the component, you can use decorative stitching and lettering.

• Print information from your home printer onto fusible fabric sheets and fuse to the back of the quilt.

• Print text onto paper, and then trace it onto muslin using a permanent marker.

• Have professional labels made.

Finish your quilt by adding a label.

Chapter Two

Super Small Swaps

In this chapter we explore small swaps. Small swaps usually consist of ten people or less, and commonly are between just two people. Small swaps are a great way to start; by focusing on a small number of items to complete, you have a little less deadline pressure. Another advantage of small swaps is the extreme amount of attention that you can give to them. You can really learn about what your swap partner likes and customize an item just for him or her.

To participate in a small swap, either join a swap group or simply ask someone if they'd like to swap items. You may find someone online whom you really admire and reach out to them, or you may already have developed a friendship with a fellow quilter. Be sure to set clear guidelines. For example, agree on the amount of money you'd like to spend on the fabric. Talk about what you'd like to swap—perhaps you both collect pin cushions and agree to make each other a unique one. Tell each other about your favorite fabrics, color preferences or anything else you'd like to get out of your swap experience.

The Hexie Table Runner Swap

There is a huge hexie-craze going on right now in the quilting world. Hexagons are a great ongoing project because they are super portable—you can work on them anywhere. Hexagons are also a wonderful way to use your fabric scraps. They are fantastic for small, quilted projects such as pillows, bags, purses and pin cushions. Be careful, though, because they are highly addictive!

To Lead This Swap, You'll Need:

MATERIALS

- 2¹/₂" English paper piecing Hexagon Template (see page 132)
- Heavy cardstock
- Scraps of colorful fabric to make hexagons
- (6) 3" light gray fabric squares (center hexagons)
- 1 yd. dark gray solid fabric
- Polyester thread for basting hexagons
- White thread for machine sewing
- 19" × 46" piece of batting
- Complementary fabric for binding

TOOLS

- Water-soluble glue stick
- Fabric scissors
- Paper scissors
- Rotary cutter
- Rotary cutting mat
- Acrylic ruler
- Iron
- Embroidery needle
- Pins
- ¼" foot for piecing
- Free motion foot for quilting

OTHER

- 5 swappers, plus you
- Envelopes
- Postage

How the Swap Works

This kind of swap can be opened to an unlimited number of participants. For our swap, we had six total swappers. All six people each made fifty hexagons, and then shipped ten hexies to each participant. Everyone received fifty hexagons in return. If you choose to include a larger number of participants, you will need to increase the number of hexagons that are made and sent.

Send each swapper their Swap Kit (see below). Explain that each swapper should make their hexies and send a certain number directly to each of the participating swappers.

The advantage of this swap is that you receive hexagons in fabrics that you don't already have. We specified modern and Japanese fabrics for our swap, but any kind of theme could be set.

Once you have received all of your hexagons, you can do whatever you'd like with them. Kerri used thirty-six of her hexagons to make this pretty table runner. She made light gray hexies to use for the center of each colorful flower. You can use your hexies any way you'd like—the sky's the limit!

Remember to share all of your hexie projects in person or through an online photo-sharing Website so everyone can see the final results.

Hexie Swap Kit

- The total number of hexies to make
- Swap instructions
- Copy of the Hexagon Template (page 132)
- Information on the size, colorway and theme for the swap
- The mailing addresses of the participating swappers
- Due date

Hexie Size: 2½" (point to point)
Finished Table Runner Size: 141½" × 42"

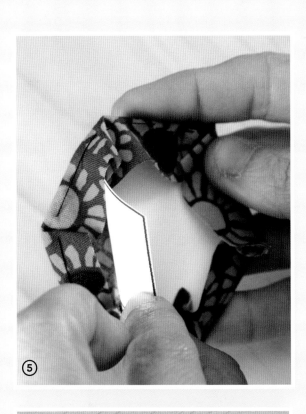

1 Cut a 3" square of fabric. Use the Fussy-Cutting Technique on page 88 to center a small motif in your square. Print the Hexagon Template provided on page 132 onto thick cardstock, or draw your own. The hexagon template measures $1^1/_4$" on each side and $2^1/_2$" from point to point. Cut out the template carefully with paper scissors.

2 Lay one of your fabric squares right-side-down. Using a water-soluble glue stick, lightly glue the hexagon to the center of the fabric square. Use fabric scissors to trim the fabric, leaving approximately $^1/_4$" of fabric around each side.

3 Baste the hexagons. Make a large knot in your polyester thread. Fold the fabric over the paper so the fabric is firm against the edge of the paper. Start basting about halfway down one of the sides, ensuring that your knot is on the paper side of your work.

4 Baste to the corner. Turn and fold the next side of the fabric over the paper, forming a tidy fold at the corner. Stitch through the folded corner to secure.

5 Continue basting and folding the corners in this manner until you get back to the start. Make three to four large stitches to anchor the thread. Carefully remove the paper from inside the hexie.

6 Cut your thread. The photo at the left shows what your basted hexie should look like, front and back.

1 After you have made or received thirty-six colorful hexagons, make six center hexagons using the 3" squares of light gray fabric. Arrange your hexagons in a pleasing way to create six flower arrangements. We put similar colors together, but you can arrange yours however you like.

2 Using a good quality polyester thread that matches your fabric color, make a small knot and anchor it with a couple of small stitches in the seam allowance of your center hexagon. Bring the needle up through one corner of the hexagon.

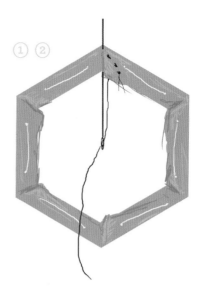

3 With right sides together, place an adjacent hexagon from the next round against the center hexagon. Holding the two hexagons together, whipstitch them together along one edge. Fasten off the thread in the seam allowance when you reach the end of the seam, but be careful not to cut the basting thread.

4 To make the round of hexagons, start another thread in the corner of a third hexagon.

5 Place this hexagon right sides together with the second hexagon, and whipstitch them together along one edge.

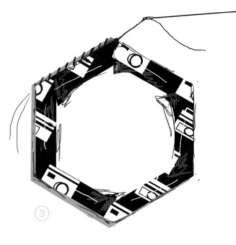

6 Open these hexagons, and place the third hexagon right sides together with the center hexagon, folding the middle hexagon as necessary. Whipstitch them together, and fasten off your thread.

7 Continue adding hexagons in the same way until you have completed your flower. It should look like this, front and back.

8 Once you have completed your flowers, iron them and take out the paper. (It is best to iron the flower before removing the paper to maintain the correct shape.)

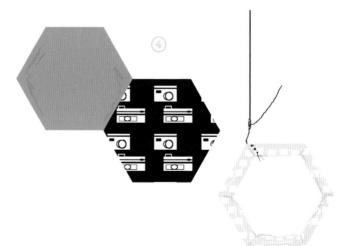

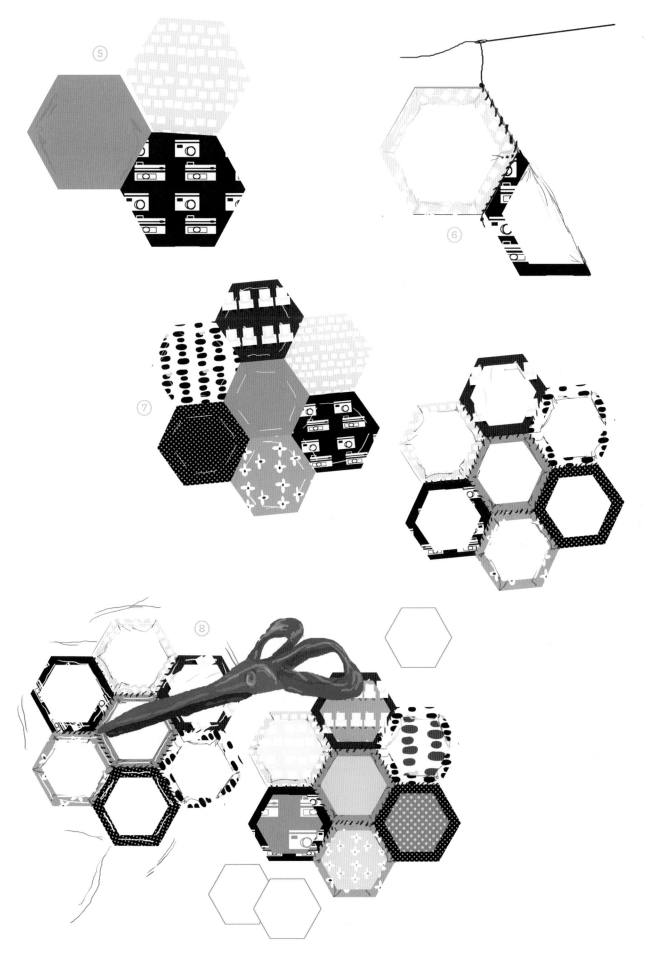

43

9 Cut two 14½" × 42" pieces of dark gray fabric. The first piece will be for the top. Put the second one aside for the bottom of the table runner.

10 Arrange the hexagon flowers on the gray fabric rectangle top until you find an arrangement you like. Pin the flowers to the fabric rectangle so they don't shift around during sewing.

Note: When Kerri put this quilt together, she laid out the flowers and took digital pictures to help decide which layout she preferred. This is a great trick for figuring out any kind of quilt layout!

11 Using a straight stitch, topstitch around each flower, staying as close to the outside edge as possible.

12 Finish the table runner by making a quilt sandwich with the batting and the second piece of gray backing. Quilt around the hexagons and bind the runner to finish.

A Tip From Melanie

"Use old bobbins of thread to baste your hexagons. The bobbins are much more portable than a spool of thread and, in my case, I have lots of wound bobbins from old clothing projects that I'll likely never use again."

Swappers:
Melanie,
Nettie,
Heather,
Tasha,
Kerri,
Angela

Quilted by:
 Kerri

The Doll Quilt Swap

Doll quilts and other small-size quilts have recently gained popularity. They are quicker to construct than bed-size quilts, offering more immediate gratification. A lot of modern quilters use doll quilts as wall hangings, often decorating their sewing area with a collection of these small quilts. They make for a great swap between two people.

WHAT'S YOUR ALL-TIME FAVORITE TYPE OF SWAP?

Allison: I think mini quilts make a fun swap, especially because they are usable. I like to hang my mini quilts all together on a wall as eye-catching artwork.

Angela: Pot holder and "mug-rug" swaps—I really enjoy using the little works of art in my everyday.

Chrissie: My favorites are home décor swaps—items that I can use immediately, like pillows.

Corey: My current favorite swap is the Pillow Talk Swap on Flickr.

John: I love all swaps, and I am a self-professed swap-aholic, but I have to say that I prefer swaps of "finished goods" (like home décor items) over block swaps. Block swaps require more work once the blocks are received, whereas a finished good can be put to immediate use.

Melanie: I like swapping blocks. Seeing a finished quilt created by the hands of many talented people from around the world is amazing.

Nova: Easy, it's the Pillow Talk Swap for me. I just can't resist that one. L.O.V.E it. Pillows are such a fun canvas to work on, and you can have so much fun with them.

Ryan: My favorite type of swap is a doll quilt swap. Designing a quilt, collecting fabrics, piecing the top, and quilting and binding it is very rewarding to my creative psyche. And you can accomplish it in a weekend. Bonus!

How the Swap Works

You only need two people to participate in this swap. If you'd like to open it to a large number of people, simply match each person involved with a partner.

Trade information with your swap partner about favorite colors and tastes in fabrics. You can provide them with pictures for inspiration if you'd like. Give them a few choices, but don't be too specific so you'll still be surprised.

Remember to share your doll quilts in person or through an online photo-sharing Website so everyone can see the final results.

Doll Quilt Swap Kit

In this swap, just send the completed doll quilt to your partner to enjoy. Lots of swappers also send a note on a pretty card or piece of stationery, some ribbon, trim or a swatch of fabic—a tiny surprise for their partner to enjoy.

A Bit of Trivia

In America during the 19th century, it was essential that a woman could sew. It was also a woman's responsibility to teach her daughters how to sew. Little girls began to sew around the age of three, usually starting with a doll quilt. Most girls enjoyed this process very much, as they liked to imitate their mother's behavior with babies.

Free Motion Embroidery Technique

1 Start by cutting out your background fabric. This block will eventually be pieced into your quilt, so plan ahead for where it will go in the completed design. (For the BICYCLES quilt, I used a muslin-colored fabric.)

On a piece of paper, draw a simple shape that is slightly smaller than the fabric you cut. If you aren't good at drawing, scan a motif from a piece of fabric and print it out at the appropriate size.

2 Place the drawing under your fabric and trace the outline with a disappearing ink fabric marker. (If you have a hard time seeing the drawing, tape the drawing and fabric to a window. The sun shining through will help you see it better.)

3 Set the background fabric aside. Cut out the main portion of the drawing from the paper sketch. (In this case, I cut out the frame of the bike.)

4 Place the shape right-side-up on top of a piece of fusible-backed fabric. Cut out the shape.

5 Iron the cutout shape in place on the background fabric over the traced outline. Make sure you have put your free motion foot on your machine and put your feed dogs down. Using black thread, "draw" over the outlines of your marker drawings. This is a free-form motion, so feel free to go back and forth over certain areas. Outline the fabric with your thread too. Your block is ready to be used in your quilt top.

①

②

③ ④

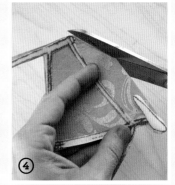
⑤

To Make Chrissie's Bicycles I Have Loved Doll Quilt, You'll Need:

MATERIALS

- Fussy-cut motifs (I used six bicycle motifs)*
- Rectangular fussy-cutting template (any size, depending on the size of your motifs)
- Variety of coordinating scrap fabrics (I used orange, turquoise and cream)
- Large scrap of cream muslin
- Double-sided fusible webbing
- White thread
- Black thread
- Coordinating embroidery threads
- 22" × 26" piece of batting
- 22" × 26" piece of fabric for backing
- Complementary fabric for binding

Munki Munki poplin pajama bottom used in sample

TOOLS

- Rotary cutter
- 18" × 24" rotary cutting mat
- Acrylic ruler
- Iron
- Scissors
- $\frac{1}{4}$" foot for piecing
- Water-soluble fabric pen
- Hand quilting needle
- Embroidery hoop

OTHER

- 1 partner
- Envelope
- Postage

Made by Chrissie, finished size: 18" × 22½"

1 Using a rectangular template and a water-soluble fabric pen, trace blocks around the motifs in your fabric. (You can use any fabric with a fun motif—it doesn't have to be bicycles.) Using the *Fussy-Cutting Technique* (see page 88), trim up your motifs.

2 I used my 18" × 24" grid cutting mat as a size reference for my overall doll quilt. Randomly arrange the fussy-cut motifs on the mat as you like. (If you don't have an 18" × 24" cutting mat, cut a piece of cardboard to the correct size, and use this as a reference when laying out your pieces.)

3 Sort through your coordinating scraps, and choose pieces that go well with your fussy-cut motifs. Begin cutting the scraps to piece next to the fussy-cut pieces. Cut the scraps the same height as the fussy-cut piece, and sew them together using a standard ¼" seam. Press.

4 Continue adding scraps of fabric that you think look good next to the fussy-cut blocks. Remember to press after sewing each seam. Try to maintain the arrangement that you created in step 3.

5 After piecing much of the top together, I decided to add a large piece of muslin to the bottom left corner of the quilt. Using appliqué and the *Free Motion Embroidery Technique* (see page 48), you will later add an embroidered image (I added a bike) to this large piece of muslin.

6 Continue piecing as you go until you have completed the top. Use the *Free Motion Embroidery Technique* to embroider your motif on the muslin block. Trim all four sides so the quilt is even. Quilt and bind.

50

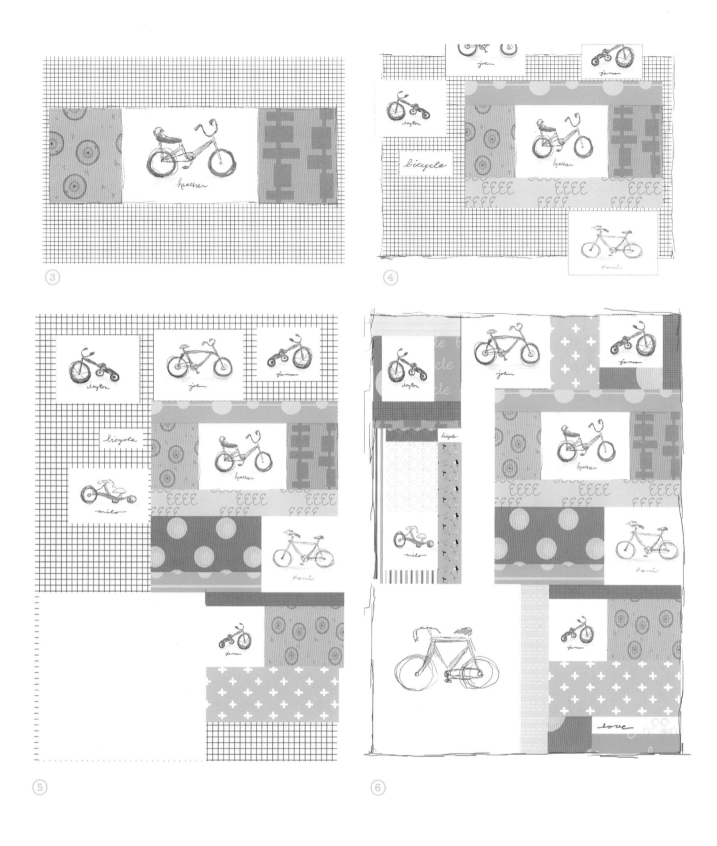

③

④

⑤

⑥

To Make John's FLIGHT OF THE BUMBLEBEE DOLL QUILT, You'll Need:

MATERIALS
- Assortment of black and yellow prints
- $1/2$ yd. white fabric
- $1/8$ yd. yellow beehive fabric
- $1/3$ yd. black dot fabric
- Double-sided fusible webbing
- White thread
- Black thread
- 24" × 28" piece of batting
- 24" × 28" piece of fabric for backing
- Complementary fabric for binding
- Bee Template (page 132)

TOOLS
- Rotary cutter
- Rotary cutting mat
- Acrylic ruler
- Iron
- Scissors
- Pencil
- $1/4$" foot for piecing
- Free motion foot for quilting

OTHER
- 1 partner
- Envelope
- Postage

Made by John, finished size: 20" × 24"

Cutting Instructions:

From assorted black and yellow prints, cut:

(24) $2^1/_2$" squares

From white fabric, cut:

(1) $6^1/_2$" × $10^1/_2$" rectangle

(24) $2^1/_2$" squares

(2) $1^1/_2$" × $18^1/_2$" strips

(2) $1^1/_2$" × $16^1/_2$" strips

From yellow beehive fabric, cut:

(2) $1^1/_2$" × $20^1/_2$" strips

(2) $1^1/_2$" × $18^1/_2$" strips

From black dot fabric, cut:

(1) $6^1/_2$" square

(2) $1^1/_2$" × $22^1/_2$" strips

(2) $1^1/_2$" × $20^1/_2$" strips

①

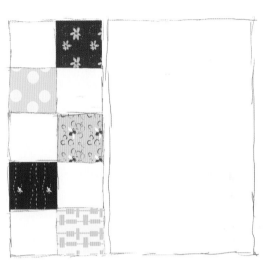

②

1 From the twenty-four white squares and the twenty-four assorted black and yellow squares, create twenty-four two-patch units by sewing each white square to a printed square. Press seams toward the printed squares.

2 Arrange five of your two-patch units in a pleasing way along one side of your $6^1/_2$" × $10^1/_2$" rectangle, alternating the placement of the printed squares as shown. Sew the five two-patch units together, creating a $4^1/_2$" × $10^1/_2$" rectangle. Sew this rectangle to the $10^1/_2$" edge of the white rectangle.

3 Repeat step 2 on the other side of your white rectangle with five additional two-patch units.

③

4 Arrange seven of your two-patch units in a pleasing way along the bottom of your quilt top, alternating the placement of the printed squares as shown in the illustration. Sew the seven two-patch units together, creating a $4^1/_2$" × $14^1/_2$" rectangle. Sew this rectangle to the bottom of your quilt top. Repeat on the top edge of the quilt top with seven additional two-patch units.

5 Sew a $1^1/_2$" × $18^1/_2$" white strip to the left and right sides of the quilt top. Then sew a $1^1/_2$" × $16^1/_2$" white strip to the top and bottom of the quilt top.

54

⑥

6 Sew a 1¹/₂" × 20¹/₂" yellow strip to the left and right sides of the quilt top. Then sew a 1¹/₂" × 18¹/₂" yellow strip to the top and bottom of the quilt top. Sew a 1¹/₂" × 22¹/₂" black dot strip to the left and right sides of the quilt top. Then sew a 1¹/₂" × 20¹/₂" black dot strip to the top and bottom of the quilt top.

7 Cut a piece of double-sided fusible webbing slightly smaller than a 6¹/₂" square. With a pencil, trace the Bee Template (found on page 132) on one side of the interfacing. Following the manufacturer's instructions, fuse one side onto the wrong side of the black dot square. Carefully cut out the bumblebee shape. Remove the other side of the adhesive, place the bumblebee in the center of your doll quilt top and fuse it into place.

8 With matching black thread, appliqué the bumblebee down by stitching around the outside the bee shape. Quilt and bind as desired. I quilted an allover meandering design with loops to imply the flight path of the bumblebee.

⑦

⑧

The Pillow Décor Swap

This swap was inspired by one of Heather and Kerri's very popular swaps called The {Urban} HOME Goods swap. This is a modern swap dedicated to creating and receiving the coolest modern and urban decorations for the home. Many people in this swap love receiving quilted pillows.

Jessica and I decided to create our own paper-pieced pillow patterns. *Paper piecing* is a traditional quilting method that is easily translated into modern-looking quilt patterns due to the precise and sharp points it can create. Paper piecing is also popular because you can make unusual shapes without needing to piece small bits of fabric.

Ask The Contributors

WHAT'S YOUR FAVORITE THING TO LISTEN TO WHILE YOU SEW?

Allison: "Midnight Train to Georgia" by Gladys Knight & the Pips . . . best song ever.

Angela: NPR podcasts.

Chrissie: I like a Pandora mix for whatever kind of mood I'm in—sometimes it's an upbeat dance mix, sometimes a mellow folk mix.

Corey: I don't usually listen to music while sewing . . . unless you can count my two-year-old banging on the piano next to me . . . she does sing every now and then.

John: Anything high energy (like the Black Eyed Peas) or mellow (like John Mayer, James Morrison, Matt Wertz or Josh Kelley)—depending on my mood.

Melanie: What I listen to when I sew depends on the level of concentration my project requires. If I'm piecing or sewing something that requires my full concentration, I like classical music playing softly in the background.

Nettie: I like to watch movies—*Pride and Prejudice* and *North and South* are my favorites.

Nova: I have an old record player and love stacking up a pile of old classics. Can't beat that scratchy, wobbly sound.

How the Swap Works

You only need two people to participate in this swap. If you'd like to open it to a large number of people, simply match each person involved with a partner.

Trade information with your swap partner about favorite colors and tastes in fabrics. You can provide them with pictures for inspiration if you'd like. Give them a few choices, but don't be too specific—that way, you'll still be surprised.

Remember to share your pillows in person or through an online photo-sharing Website so everyone can see the final results.

Pillow Décor Swap Kit

In this swap, just send the completed quilted pillowcase for your partner to enjoy.

Note: Most people do not send the pillow form along with the pillowcase. Pillow forms are usually reasonably priced at craft stores; it's usually more expensive to mail the pillow form than to send just the pillowcase.

About Paper Piecing

Although paper piecing is a traditional quilting technique, it has been revived by modern quilters. Paper-pieced blocks are made by sewing pieces of fabric onto a paper foundation, which is stitched through and torn away after sewing. Stitching onto the paper provides a temporary stabilizer for the tiny fabric pieces. Paper piecing is a very popular form of quilting because, if it's done correctly, the blocks are perfect, despite the tiny size of the patches.

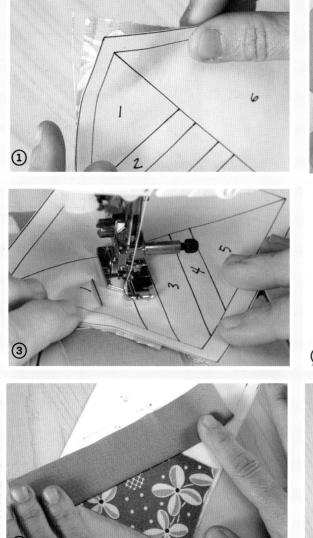

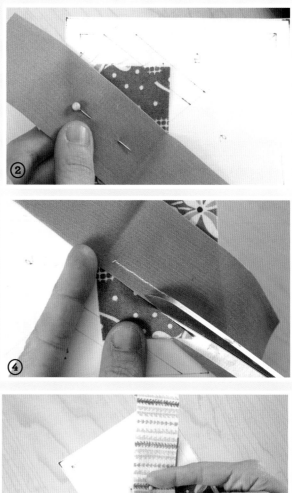

1 Before you start sewing, set your stitch length to approximately 1.0. Print or draw your pattern onto a lightweight paper. Pin space 1 fabric on the backside of the paper pattern, right side facing out. Make sure that your fabric sufficiently covers space 1 and the outside edge seam allowances on your pattern.

2 Pin on the space 2 fabric, placing it right sides together with the first piece. When the line between space 1 and space 2 is stitched, fabric 2 will open and should cover all of space 2.

3 With the drawn pattern side up, stitch on the line between space 1 and space 2.

4 Trim the excess fabric ¼" away from the stitched line to create a seam allowance.

5 Press the top fabric open.

6 Add your next fabric strip onto the back and stitch on the line between space 2 and space 3. Trim your ¼" seam allowance, and press open. Repeat this process until all of the sections of your pattern are complete. Press well. Repeat this process until all of your blocks are complete.

7 Trim all of your blocks on the outer line (this will give you a ¼" seam allowance).

8 Remove the paper from the back of your blocks.

To Make Chrissie's SEWING WITH SELVAGES PILLOW, You'll Need:

MATERIALS

- 4 sheets of lightweight paper
- 4 identical pieces of selvages or 4 identical fabric ribbons (each at least 12½" long)
- A large assortment of selvages (from 4"–12" in length)*
- White glue or gluestick
- White thread
- 21" square of batting
- 21" square of muslin
- 2 pieces of fabric, each measuring 17" × 10" (backing)
- (1) 16" square pillow form

If you don't have enough selvages to do the entire pillow, use regular fabric strips.

TOOLS

- Rotary cutter
- Rotary cutting mat
- Acrylic ruler
- Iron
- Scissors
- ¼" foot for piecing
- Pins
- Free motion foot for quilting

OTHER

- 1 partner
- Envelope
- Postage

Made by Chrissie, finished size: 16" × 16"

1 To make a 16" × 16" pillow, cut four $8^3/_4$" × $8^3/_4$" squares of lightweight paper, such as copy paper or children's drawing paper. Working with the identical selvages or fabric ribbon, lightly glue a strip of selvage or ribbon from corner to corner on each square of paper.

2 Dig through your selvages and trim them to varying sizes in width. I cut mine from $^1/_2$"–$1^1/_2$" in width.

3 Reduce your stitch length to 1.4–1.6. The small stitches will perforate your paper, allowing you to remove the paper easily later. Starting with your first square, begin sewing on your selvage strips. The first strip needs to be long enough to cover the length of the paper right next to the piece glued on the diagonal. With right sides together, align one edge of the selvage strip with the center strip. Sew down the edge with a scant $^1/_4$" seam, if possible. (Some of my selvages were so tiny that I had to sew right next to the edge of the fabrics.)

4 Press the strip open. Repeat to sew a selvage strip to the other side of the center strip.

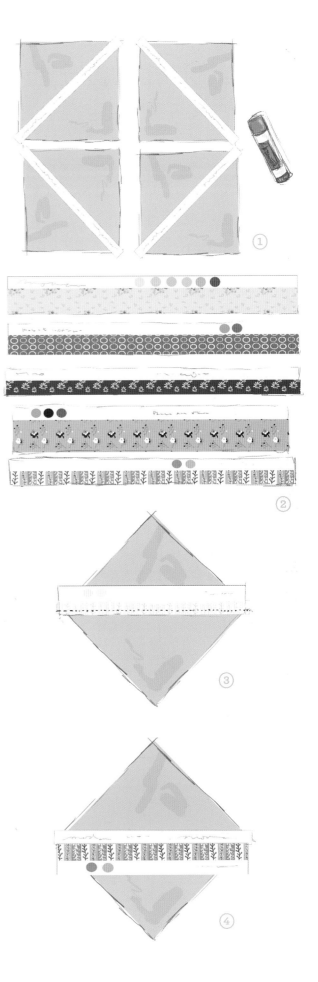

5 Continue sewing one strip to the previous strip, right sides together, and pressing open until you have covered the entire square.

6 Turn your square over with the paper-side up, and trim the excess fabric off of all four sides. Fold the paper along the sewn lines and carefully remove all the paper. Repeat this process to complete the other three squares.

7 Arrange the blocks as you like. I liked the look of a conventional diamond. Sew the top two blocks together using a ¼" seam, and then press. Do the same to join the bottom two blocks.

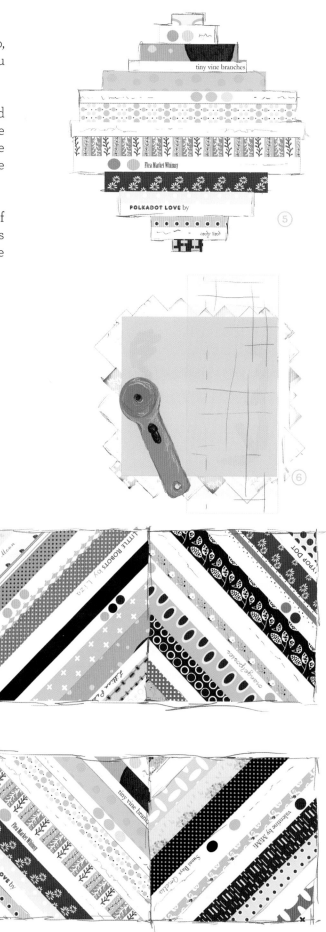

62

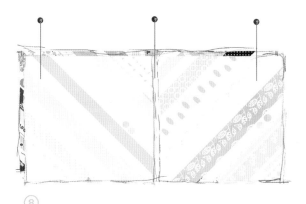

(8)

8 Place the bottom and top halves right sides together and pin. Sew together using a standard $^1/_4$" seam. Press open and trim your block to 17" square.

9 Make your quilt sandwich with the selvages on top, muslin on the bottom and batting in between.

10 Quilt using your free motion foot. I used free-form circle quilting, which created a nice juxtaposition against the straight lines of the fabrics. Once you are finished quilting, trim your pillow top to 17" square.

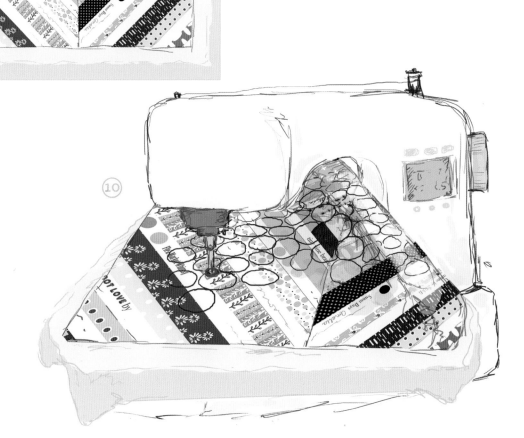

(9)

(10)

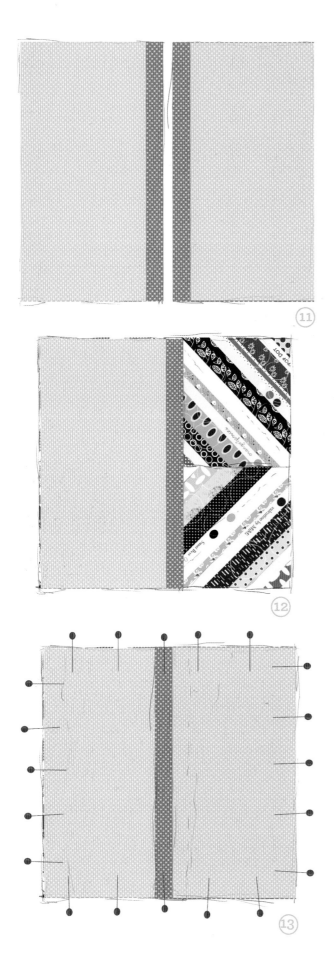

11 To make the back of the pillow, cut two 17" × 10" pieces of matching fabric. On both pieces, fold one long edge under ¹/₂" to the wrong side and press in place. Fold under ¹/₂" a second time and press. Straight stitch the hem in place all the way down the fold on both pieces.

12 Place your pillow top right-side-up. Place one of the back pieces right-side-down on top of the pillow top, outer edges matching. The hemmed edge should be in the center.

13 Place the other piece the same way on the other side. The hemmed pieces will overlap in the middle. Pin all the way around. Sew around all four sides of the pillow, using a ¹/₄" seam allowance.

14 Turn the pillow right-side-out and press to flatten the seams. Insert the pillow form.

MATERIALS

- 12 copies of Pattern A block (page 132)
- 12 copies of Pattern B block (page 133)
- ¼ yd. solid fabric* (space 2 and space 4)
- ¼ yd. striped fabric** (space 3)
- ½ yd. floral print fabric** (space 6)
- ⅓ yd. patterned fabric** (space 1 and space 5)
- ½ yd. fabric for backing, facings and ties
- 16" × 28" piece of batting
- 16" × 28" piece of muslin
- (1) 12" × 24" pillow form

*Kona Sage used in sample

**Hope Valley line by Denyse Schmidt used in sample

TOOLS

- Rotary cutter
- Rotary cutting mat
- Acrylic ruler
- Iron
- Scissors
- Embroidery needle
- Straight pins
- ¼" foot for piecing
- Walking foot for quilting

OTHER

- 1 partner
- Envelope
- Postage

Made by Jessica, finished size: 12" × 24"

1 Using the *Paper Piecing Technique* (see page 58), paper piece twelve A blocks and twelve B blocks so you have twenty-four total blocks. Refer to the Materials List on page 65 for fabric placement.

2 Lay out the blocks in four rows, as shown. Stitch the blocks together in rows using a standard ¼" seam. Press the seam allowances open. Sew the rows together to complete your pillow top.

3 Make your quilt sandwich by basting together the pillow top on top, batting in the middle and muslin on the bottom. Quilt the sandwich with straight lines. Trim excess batting and backing fabric even with the edges of the pillow top.

4 Use the ½ yd. piece of fabric to make the backing, ties and facings. To make the facings, cut two 12½" × 6" pieces of fabric. On both pieces, fold one long edge under ½" to the wrong side and press in place. Straight stitch the folded edge in place all the way down the length on both pieces.

5 To make the ties, cut two strips of fabric measuring 2½" × 22". Cut them in half to create four 2½" × 11" ties. Fold them all in half lengthwise, wrong sides together, and pin. On one end of each tie, draw an angled line. Stitch across the length of each tie and along the drawn angled line. Trim the fabric ¼" away from the stitched angle, turn the ties right side out and press.

6 Cut a backing piece 12½" × 24½". Place it right-side-up on a flat surface. Place two ties on the right-hand side of the backing, one 3" up from the bottom, and one 3" down from the top, aligning the raw edges of the ties with the raw edges of the backing. Pin and stitch along the raw edges of the ties to secure them to the backing.

7 With right sides together, place the raw edge of one facing rectangle on the right edge of the backing and pin. Using a standard ¼" seam, stitch along the raw edge to attach the facing piece to the backing.

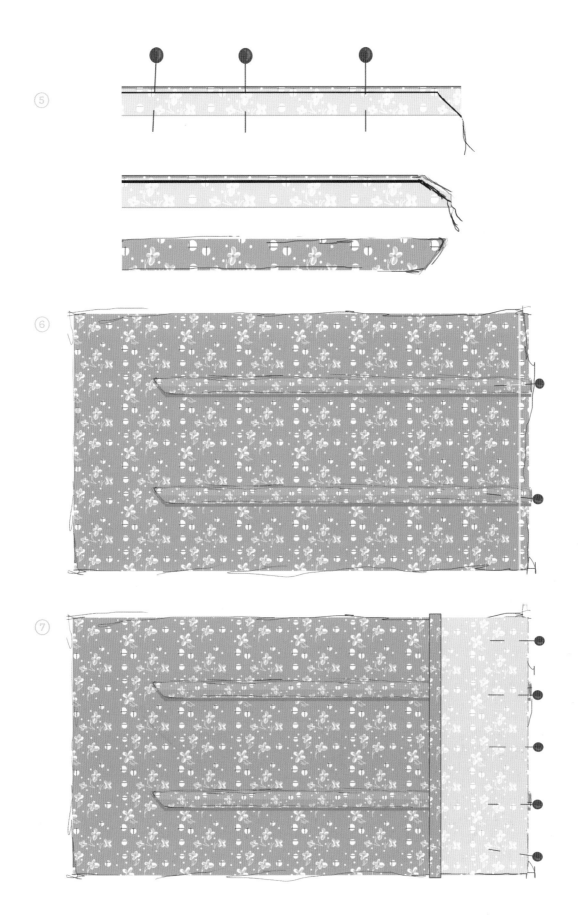

8 Press the seam toward the facing, and topstitch the seam open. Fold the facing piece to the wrong side of the backing so the two pieces are wrong sides together. Press again.

9 Place the other two ties on the right-hand side of the front of the pillow, one 3" up from the bottom, and one 3" down from the top, aligning the raw edges of the ties with the raw edges of the pillow top. Pin and stitch the ties to the pillow top.

10 In the same way as you added a facing piece to the backing, add the second facing piece to the right-hand side of the pillow top. Press toward the facing and topstitch the seam open. Don't wrap the facing piece to the back of the pillow top.

11 With the pillow top right-side-up, place the backing on top, right-side-down, aligning the left-hand raw edges (not the facing edges). Pin along the bottom, top and left-hand edges.

12 Flip the bottom facing over the right-hand edge and pin on top of the other facing. This encloses all of the raw edges when the pillow cover is turned right-side-out.

13 Stitch ¼" from the edge around three sides of the pillow (top, bottom and left-hand edges).

14 Turn the pillow case right-side-out, insert your pillow form and tie the ties.

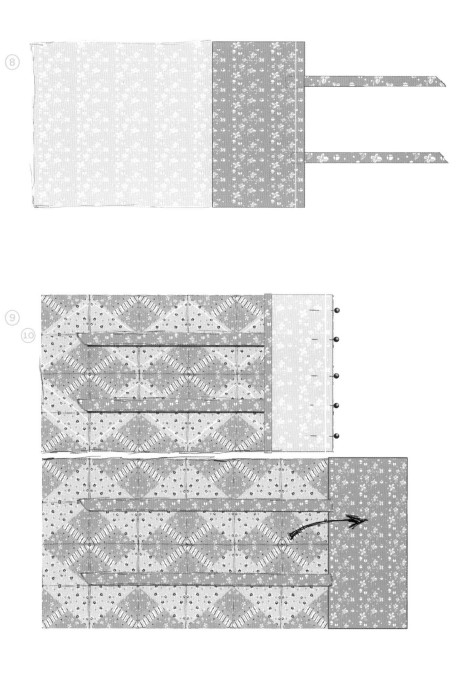

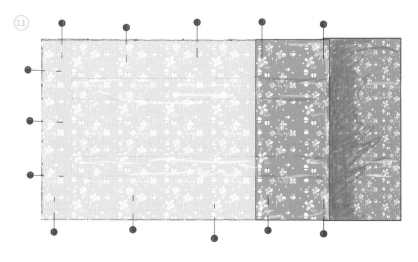

68

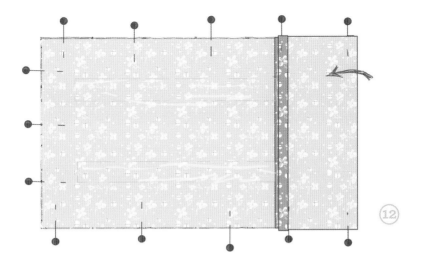

⑫

⑬

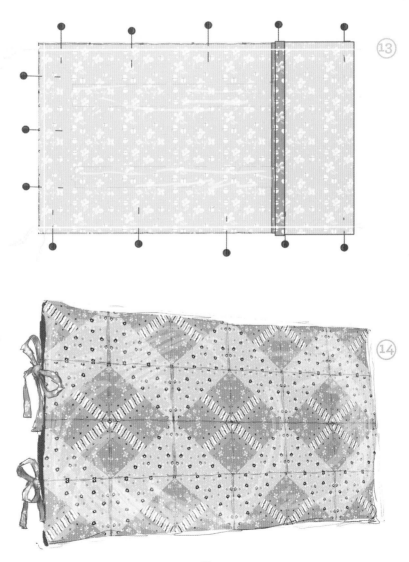

⑭

Chapter Three

Marvelous Medium Swaps

We're moving now into some medium-sized swaps. Medium swaps usually consist of 10–25 people. The most common types of medium-sized swaps are quilting-bee swaps (see page 9) and block-of-the-month swaps.

In a block-of-the-month swap, you need twelve swappers including yourself. Each participant is assigned his or her own month. When it is your month, ask the other eleven swappers to make you a particular type of block. Tell them the exact size and dimensions that the finished block should be. Give specifics on the color scheme or the exact pattern you'd like them to use. If you want everyone to use a particular type of fabric, you need to send them the fabric. If it's a block that is not widely available, send everyone a copy of the pattern. At the end of your month, you will receive eleven original blocks. After you have made yours, you will have enough to make your own special quilt top. Then it's on to the next person's block.

Medium-sized swaps are a wonderful way to develop long-term friendships since you will be working with the same group of people for an extended period of time. So much originality and creativity is usually discovered in this type of swap. It's always fun to see what people come up with.

A Few of My Favorite Things Swap

This quilt is a modern take on redwork. Embroidery in quilting has become popular again, and I wanted to work this traditional technique into a modern quilt. Inspired by a similar project by fellow contributor, Nova, I came up with nine drawings of some of my favorite things that I thought would make for an interesting composition in a redwork quilt.

To Lead This Swap, You'll Need:

MATERIALS
• 9 sheets of white paper

• 9 favorite things as inspiration (or use the embroidery patterns found on pages 130–132)

• 15 complementary fat quarters* (divvied up 9 ways)

• (9) 8" × 10" pieces of off-white solid fabric

• 9 matching skeins of red embroidery thread

• Off-white thread

• 51" square of batting

• 51" square of fabric for backing

• Complementary fabric for binding

*City Weekend fabric line by Oliver + S used in sample

TOOLS
• Pencil

• Water-soluble fabric pen

• Rotary cutter

• Rotary cutting mat

• Acrylic ruler

• Iron

• Embroidery needle

• Scissors

• ¼" foot for piecing

• Walking foot for quilting

• Black fine-tipped marker

OTHER
• 8 swappers, plus you

• Envelopes

• Postage

How the Swap Works

You need eight swappers plus yourself to make a total of nine blocks.

Draw simple images of nine of your favorite things on a piece of paper in black marker. Each image should be no bigger than 7" x 9", or use the embroidery patterns from the sample quilt (pages 130–132).

Send each swapper their Swap Kit (see below). Ask them to make a block using the instructions and the drawing provided, and to return the block to you on a specified date.

When I received the blocks back from my swappers, I laid them out next to each other in various ways until I was pleased with the arrangement. I then stitched the blocks together using a standard ¼" seam. After sewing the quilt top together, I used simple straight-line quilting with an off-white thread—I really wanted the embroidered centers to be the focal point, and I didn't want to quilt over them.

Take turns like this until each member of your swap group has had a chance to make their own special quilt representing his or her favorite things.

Remember to share your finished quilts in person or through an online photo-sharing Website so everyone can see the final results.

A Few of My Favorite Things Swap Kit

• (1) 8" x 10" piece of off-white solid fabric

• (9) fabric strips, each cut from a different fabric fat quarter (see step 2 on page 76 for strip sizes)

• (1) skein of red embroidery thread

• (1) of your "favorite things" drawings

• Block instructions

• Your return address

• Due date

Block Size: 16" x 16"

Finished Quilt Size: 47" x 47"

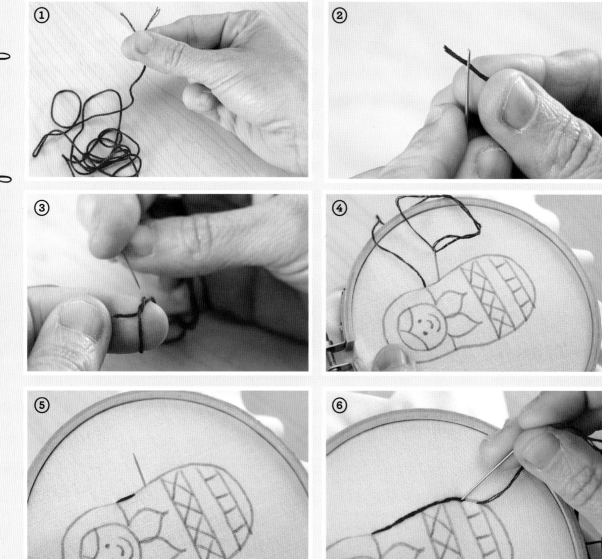

Backstitch

1 To make your embroidered piece, you will use a basic embroidering stitch called a *backstitch*. You are aiming for a row of small, evenly sized stitches that imitate a drawn line. First, choose your embroidery thread color. Cut your piece of embroidery floss about 18" long. Embroidery floss has six strands and is usually used two or three strands at a time, depending on how thick you want your stitched line to appear.

2 Work the cut end of the floss through the eye of the needle and pull it through. Make sure you are using a needle appropriate for embroidery. The needle should be only slightly thicker at the eye than the thickness of your thread, making a hole in the fabric that the thread can pass through easily.

3 Wrap the end of the thread around your pointer finger, pass the thread through the loop and tie a knot.

4 Working from right to left, stitch up through the fabric, move to the left about ⅛", and push the needle back though the fabric.

5 Move to the left about ⅛", stitch back up through the fabric and then push the needle through the fabric where your previous stitch ended, completing the line.

6 Continue working backstitches along your drawn line.

74

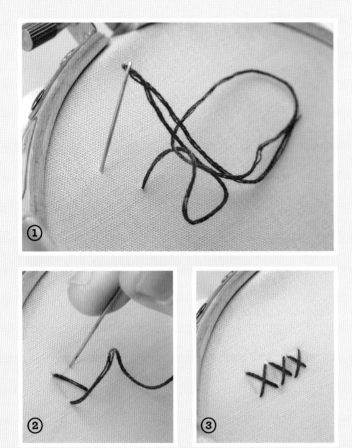

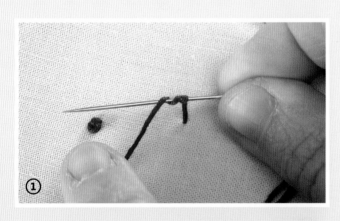

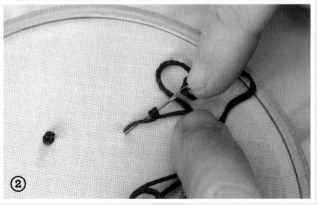

Cross-Stitch

1 Separate your floss, using as many strands as you'd like depending on desired thickness. Thread a needle and knot one end of the embroidery floss. Come up through your fabric so the knot is on the wrong side of the fabric. Stitch back down through the fabric above and to the left of the first stitch to create the first cross of your cross-stitch.

2 Stitch back up through the fabric below the previous stitch. Stitch back down through the fabric to complete the cross-stitch.

3 Continue making cross-stitches as desired to embellish your design.

French Knot

1 In the same way described above, thread a needle and knot one end. Stitch up through your fabric. Wrap the thread around your needle three to four times, wrapping very close to the fabric.

2 Holding the wraps on the needle, push the needle down through the fabric right next to the spot you came up. Hold the wraps on the top of the fabric as you slowly pull the thread through. The wraps will form a knot on the top of the fabric.

3 Continue making French knots as desired to embellish your design.

1 Tape your drawing to a table. Tape the 8" × 10" piece of off-white fabric over the drawing, right-side-up, making sure to leave at least ½" all the way around the image. Use a water-soluble fabric pen to trace the image onto the fabric.

2 For each block, cut nine strips, each strip from a different fabric. Cut the strips for one block in the following sizes, and press them well:
(2) $2^1/_2$" × $2^1/_2$"
(1) $2^1/_2$" × 8"
(2) $2^1/_2$" × 10"
(1) $2^1/_2$" × 12"
(2) $2^1/_2$" × 14"
(1) $2^1/_2$" × 16"

3 Using a standard $^1/_4$" seam, sew a $2^1/_2$" × 8" strip to the left side of the embroidery piece. Press open.

4 Sew the $2^1/_2$" blocks to the $2^1/_2$" × 10" strips. Press open.

5 Sew the pieced strips to the top and bottom of the embroidery block, with the pieced squares on the left-hand side. Press open.

6 Sew the $2^1/_2$" × 12" strip to the left side of the block. Press open.

7 Sew the $2^1/_2$" × 14" strip to the top of the block. Press open.

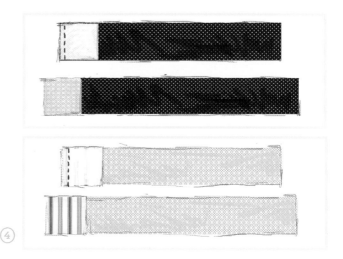

⑤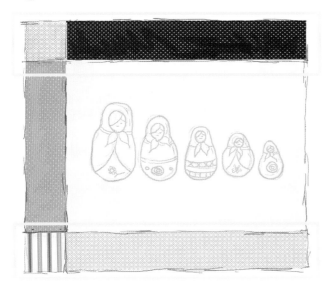

⑥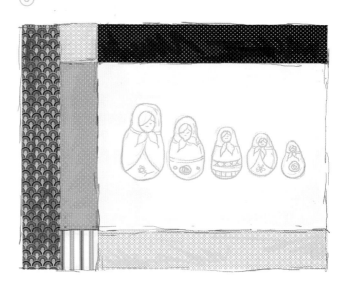

⑦

8 Sew the 2½" × 16" strip to the right side of the block. Press open.

9 Sew the 2½" × 18" strip to the bottom of the block. Press open.

10 Using the red embroidery thread, embroider your center piece. I recommend using a hoop to hold your fabric taut as you embroider.

Note: If you are more comfortable embroidering your piece before you sew the block, that is fine as well.

11 Press well. Your block should measure 16" square.

12 Once you receive all of your blocks, sew them together in three rows of three blocks. Quilt and bind.

A Bit of Trivia

Redwork embroidery has quite a history. As the Victorian trend for making crazy quilts subsided, redwork embroidery took its place. Although the popularity of redwork embroidery peaked around the turn of the century, it wasn't a new craft. Beginning in the 1880s, women had been willing to pay extra for a thread color called "Turkey Red" because, unlike most colors, it was colorfast. At first, redwork was done on a variety of useful household items, but not on quilts. It wasn't until the turn of the century that women began to use redwork embroidery for bedcoverings.

Swappers: Heather, Kerri, John, Chrissie, Crystal, Nova, Corey, Jessica, Jennifer

Quilted by: Chrissie

The Diamond Block Swap

This quilt is inspired by traditional Amish quilts. Amish quilt designs are based on the belief that art is not separate from day-to-day life and that beauty is a part of function—a concept that can be an inspiration to all quilters. This quilt exemplifies the beauty of combining a traditional quilt pattern with modern fabrics.

To Lead This Swap, You'll Need:

MATERIALS
- Clear or transparent template plastic
- 9 complementary, patterned fat quarters*
- $2/3$ yd. of blue solid fabric**
- $2/3$ yd. of brown solid fabric**
- Light brown thread
- 33" square of cotton batting
- 33" square of fabric for backing
- Complementary fabric for binding

*Little Folks fabric line (in voile) by Anna Maria Horner used in sample

**Anna Maria Horner solids used in sample

TOOLS
- Rotary cutter
- Rotary cutting mat
- Acrylic ruler
- Iron
- Scissors
- Pins
- Permanent marker
- $1/4$" foot for piecing
- Free motion foot for quilting
- Utility knife
- Disappearing ink fabric pen

OTHER
- 8 swappers, plus you
- Envelopes
- Postage

How the Swap Works

You'll need eight swappers plus yourself to make a total of nine blocks.

Send each swapper their Swap Kit (see below). Ask them to make a block using the instructions and to return the block to you on a specified date.

I had already decided how I wanted to arrange this quilt when I mailed the packages, alternating the brown and blue solid stripping. I stitched the blocks together using a standard $1/4$" seam. After sewing the quilt top together, I decided to use a swirl quilt pattern to break up the hard lines of the diamonds.

Take turns making diamond blocks for each swap member with his or her preferred fabrics.

Remember to share your finished quilts in person or through an online photo-sharing Website so everyone can see the final results.

Diamond Block Swap Kit

- 1 fat quarter
- 10" x 14" piece of one solid fabric (five swappers get blue, four swappers get brown)
- Block instructions
- Your return address
- Due date

Block Size: 10" x 10"

Finished Quilt Size: 29" x 29"

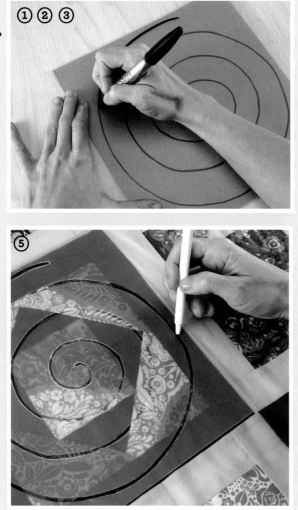

1 Decide what size you want your quilt stencil to be. I've decided on 9½" square here because that is the size of my block after they are all sewn together. Cut a piece of template plastic to that size.

2 With paper and pencil, sketch out the quilt design you'd like to make. Draw your own free-form design, or use a free online template or one from a book of quilting patterns. Make sure your design isn't larger than the template piece you cut in step 1.

3 Lay the clear template plastic over your drawing and trace the design carefully with a wide permanent marker—ideally the drawn line will measure ⅛" wide. Your lines, when cut, will form the shape of the motif.

Note: When you draw the lines of full shapes, such as circles and hearts, make sure your lines are not completely connected. You must leave at least 1" of space somewhere on the outline of each motif to ensure that you don't cut out a circle, triangle or rectangle when you are cutting out your design.

4 Place the template onto your cutting mat. Using a sharp utility knife, begin cutting the lines that form your stencil. You will cut along both sides of the drawn line. Cut a few inches at a time, remove the plastic and continue.

5 Starting in the middle of your quilt, lay your template over the first block. Using a disappearing ink fabric pen, trace your stencil onto the block. If you are going to complete the whole quilt in one day, draw your stencils in all of the blocks. If not, just do one at a time.

6 Use your free motion foot to quilt over the stenciled lines.

1 From the patterned fat quarter, cut a 4" × 4" middle square.

2 From the solid fabric, cut four triangles that measure $4^3/_4$" on the bottom and $3^1/_2$" on each side.

3 With right sides together, pin two triangles to opposite sides of the square, aligning the long edge of the triangle with the side of the square. The triangle will hang over the edges slightly; center it as best you can. Using a $1/_4$" seam, sew the triangles to the square. Press the triangles open.

4 In the same way, pin and sew the other two triangles to the remaining sides of the square. Press the triangles open.

①

②

A Note About Using Voile Fabric

For this quilt, we used voile fabric instead of standard 100% cotton quilting fabric. Compared to quilting-weight cotton, voile is lighter weight, more sheer and ideal for clothing, but you can also use it for quilting. One advantage to quilting with voile is the softness and livability of this fabric. People describe quilts made from voile as "buttery soft." If you decide to quilt with voile, I would advise sewing a little slower than you normally would. Switch to a smaller needle, like a 9 (or 11 at the largest). Using a walking foot will also help stabilize the fabric as you sew. You could also iron the fabric to a light-weight fusible interfacing to add "sturdiness" to the fabric.

③

④

83

5 Trim the square to measure 5¼" on all sides.

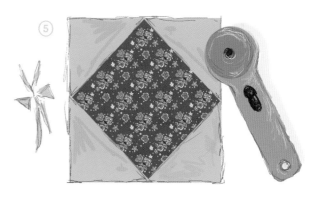

6 From your patterned fabric, cut four triangles that measures 6¾" on the bottom and 4¾" on each side.

7 Sew these four triangles to the outside of the square in the same way. Press open and trim the block to 8½" square.

8 From the solid fabric, cut four 2" × 8" strips. Sew a strip to the top and bottom of the square. Press open and trim the ends of the strips even with the sides of the block. Sew the remaining strips to the sides of the block. Press open.

9 Trim the finished block to measure 10" square.

10 Once you receive all of your blocks, sew them together in three rows of three blocks, alternating background colors as shown on page 85. Try making your own quilt stencil using the technique on page 82. Quilt and bind.

Swappers: Angela, Ryan, Tasha,
Chrissie, Jennifer, Nova,
Jessica, John, Nettie

Quilted by: Chrissie

The Scrapbuster Swap

I am very partial to a nice, colorful pile of fabric scraps. A lot of quilters, including myself, have scrap bins full of bits of fabric that they can't part with. I love the challenge of finding fun things to make with my scraps. When I saw Corey's *Stashbuster* tutorials on her blog, I fell in love! I adore the way the dark gray fabric contrasts with all the tiny pieces of colored fabric. It's such a modern look, and I get so much satisfaction knowing that all of those tiny pieces I saved were not wasted.

To Lead This Swap, You'll Need:

MATERIALS
- Transparent template plastic
- Large assortment of scrap fabrics
- 1⅓ yds. of dark gray solid fabric*
- Dark gray thread
- 41" square of cotton batting
- 41" square of fabric for backing
- Complementary fabric for binding

Kona charcoal used in sample

TOOLS
- Disappearing ink marker
- Rotary cutter
- Rotary cutting mat
- Acrylic ruler
- Iron
- Scissors
- ¼" foot for piecing
- Walking foot for quilting

OTHER
- 8 swappers, plus you
- Envelopes
- Postage

How the Swap Works

You need eight swappers plus yourself to make a total of nine blocks.

Corey designed this block in two different ways. Ask four of your swappers to create Block 1, and ask five of them to create Block 2.

Send each swapper their Swap Kit (see below). Ask them to make the block using the fabrics provided. Tell them to feel free to add their own little scraps if they'd like, and ask that the block be returned to you by a specified date.

Corey was the swap leader on this one, so when she received all the blocks back, she assembled the quilt in three rows of three blocks, alternating Block 1 with Block 2 using a standard ¼" seam. After sewing the quilt top together, she quilted the project with a modern, straight-line pattern using her walking foot.

Take turns like this until all the members of your swap group have had a chance to make their own quilt using their scrap stash.

Remember to share your finished quilts in person or through an online photo-sharing Website so everyone can see the final results.

Scrapbuster Swap Kit

- 13" square of dark gray fabric to make strips
- Nice collection of scrap fabrics
- Block instructions (four swappers should make Block 1 and five swappers should make Block 2)
- Your return address
- Due date

Block Size: 12½" x 12½"
Finished Quilt Size: 36½" x 36½"

Fussy-Cutting Technique

1 From a piece of clear template plastic, cut a piece that measures the size of your desired piece. (For this project, cut a $1\frac{1}{2}$" square.)

2 As you go through your fabric scraps, look for areas that you'd like to have as your focal point in each block. Lay your template on the fabric until you find the area you want to focus on. Remember that when you piece the block, you will lose $\frac{1}{4}$" on all sides in the seam allowances, so try to make sure the focus point is $\frac{1}{4}$" away from all edges of the template.

3 Use a disappearing ink marker to trace around the outside of your template.

4 Use your rotary cutter and ruler or scissors to cut out your squares.

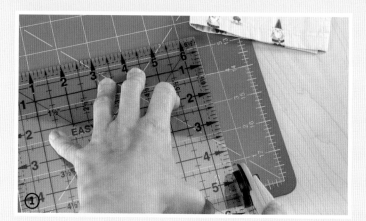

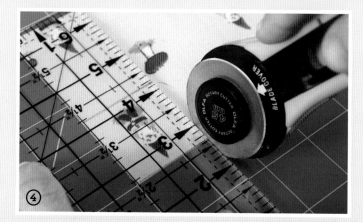

①

②

③

④

Make Block 1

1 Cut a $3\frac{1}{2}$" square out of the dark gray fabric. Using the *Fussy-Cutting Technique* on page 88, cut out forty-eight $1\frac{1}{2}$" squares from the scrap fabric.

2 To make the first colorful border, sew two strips of three $1\frac{1}{2}$" squares. Press them open. Sew these pieced strips to the top and bottom of the gray square using a standard $\frac{1}{4}$" seam. Press them open.

3 In the same way, sew and press two strips of five $1\frac{1}{2}$" squares. Sew these to the sides of the gray square. Press them open.

4 To make the first gray border, cut two $1\frac{1}{2}$" × $5\frac{1}{2}$" strips from the gray fabric. Sew these to the top and bottom of the block. Press them open.

Quilt Variations

So many different options are possible for this quilt. I think it would be beautiful to pick a color scheme for the fabric scraps and use a contrasting color for the solid. It would also be really fun to pick a fabric theme. For example, use fabric scraps that only have polka dots on them or scraps based on a holiday theme. The possibilities are endless.

5 Cut two $1^1/_2" \times 7^1/_2"$ strips from the gray fabric. Sew these to the sides of the block. Press them open.

6 To make the second colorful border, sew two strips of seven $1^1/_2"$ squares. Sew these to the top and bottom of the block and press them open. Sew two strips made up of nine $1^1/_2"$ squares. Sew these to the sides of the block and press them open.

7 To make the final gray border, cut two $2" \times 9^1/_2"$ strips from the gray fabric. Sew them to the top and bottom of the block. Press them open. Cut two $2" \times 12^1/_2"$ strips from the gray fabric. Sew these to the sides of the block and press them open. Your finished block should measure $12^1/_2"$ square.

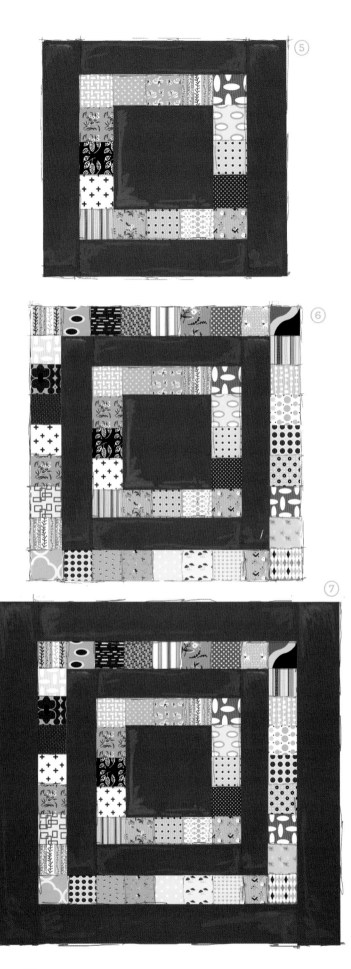

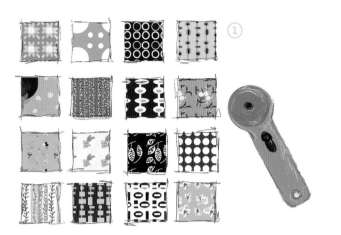

①

②

③

1 Using the *Fussy-Cutting Technique* on page 88, cut eighty-eight 1½" squares from the fabric scraps. Arrange sixteen of these squares into four rows of four squares.

2 Sew the squares together in rows. Press seam allowances of the first row to the left, the second row to the right, the third row to the left and the fourth row to the right. This will nest your seams perfectly and align all of the squares. Sew the rows together and press. Your middle section will measure 4½" square.

3 To make the first gray border, cut two 1½" × 4½" strips from the gray fabric. Sew these strips to the top and bottom of the center block. Press them open. Cut two 1½" × 6½" strips from the gray fabric and sew them to the sides. Press them open. Your block will now measure 6½" square.

4 To make the first colorful border, sew two strips of six $1^1/_2$" squares. Sew these to the top and bottom of the block. Press them open. Sew two strips of eight $1^1/_2$" squares. Sew these to the sides of the block. Press them open. Your block should now measure $8^1/_2$" square.

5 To make the second gray border, cut two $1^1/_2$" × $8^1/_2$" strips from the gray fabric. Sew them to the top and bottom of the block. Press them open. Cut two $1^1/_2$" × $10^1/_2$" strips from the gray fabric. Sew them to the sides of the block. Press them open. Your block should now measure $10^1/_2$" square.

6 To make the final colorful border, sew two strips made of ten $1^1/_2$" squares. Attach these to the top and bottom. Press them open. Sew two strips made of twelve $1^1/_2$" squares. Attach these to the sides. Press them open. Your finished block should now measure $12^1/_2$" square.

7 Once you have made and received all of your blocks, sew them into three rows of three blocks each, alternating Block 1 with Block 2 as shown on page 93. Use any extra scraps to piece a back, if desired (see pages 28–29). Quilt and bind.

Swappers: Nova, Jennifer, Chrissie, John, Corey, Melanie, Crystal, Ryan, Jessica

Quilted by: Corey

The Curvy Block Swap

Sewing circles and curves seems intimidating to a lot of quilters. I'll be honest here—a few of the quilters involved in this swap weren't overly excited about making these blocks. However, I must assure you that circles and curves are not nearly as difficult as they look, and the end result is well worth the effort.

To Lead This Swap, You'll Need:

MATERIALS

- (12) ¼ yd. cuts of complementary fabrics* (divvied up 12 ways)
- 1 ¾ yd. of white fabric** (divvied up 12 ways)
- Curvy Block Templates (found on pages 133–135)
- 1 yd. of dark gray fabric for sashing***
- White thread
- Double-sided fusible webbing
- 48" × 62" piece of cotton batting
- 48" × 62" piece of fabric for backing
- Complementary fabric for binding

Tufted Tweets fabric line from Robert Kaufman used in sample

**Kona white used in sample*

***Kona charcoal used in sample*

TOOLS

- Rotary cutter
- Rotary cutting mat
- Acrylic ruler
- Water-soluble marker
- Iron
- Scissors
- Pins
- ¼" foot for piecing
- Free motion foot for quilting
- Easy Dresden Ruler (1 block only)

OTHER

- 11 swappers, plus you
- Envelopes
- Postage

How the Swap Works

You need eleven swappers plus yourself to make a total of twelve blocks.

This type of swap typically consists of twelve quilters and lasts for one year. Every month, one participant has the chance to request a certain type of block. Other participants make the requested block and send it to that month's swap leader by the end of the month. The group's leader rotates every month until each swapper has had a chance to request blocks.

When it is your month, send each swapper their Swap Kit (see below). I let each quilter choose their own block pattern as long as it had circular or curved pieces, but you can send a specific block pattern if you'd like. You can ask your group to use scraps or some fabric from their own stash, but I sent each member of my group a block of white fabric to use for consistent backgrounds and an assortment of fabrics from my ¼ yds. of complementary fabrics. Ask the participants to make and return the block to you by a specified date.

After receiving the blocks, I sashed them with a dark gray fabric for strong contrast and to highlight each individual block. After sewing the quilt top together using a standard ¼" seam, I decided to have a professional quilter tackle the extensive quilting for me.

Remember to share your finished quilts in person or through an online photo-sharing Website so everyone can see the final results.

Note: Some quilters chose appliqué as the technique for their circles, while some sewed them on the machine using curved piecing.

Curvy Block Swap Kit

- Assortment of complementary fabrics (totaling approximately ¼ yd.)
- 13" square of white solid fabric
- Block instructions and template (if applicable) and finished block size
- Your return address
- Due date

Block Size: 12" x 12"
Finished Quilt Size: 44" x 58"

95

Piecing Curves Technique

1 Use a curved template and a water-soluble marker to trace both parts of the curved template onto your fabric, or pin the templates directly to the fabric.

2 Use super-sharp fabric scissors to cut out the shapes. (The templates in this book include $1/4$" seam allownace. If you use templates from another source, make sure they include the seam allowance; if not, cut $1/4$" outside of the drawn line.)

3 Cut tiny snips all the way along the curved side of the inside curved piece (white piece). The snips should be about $1/4$" apart and $1/8$" deep. This allows you to stretch the piece while stitching your curves together. Do not snip the outside curved piece (printed piece).

4 Pin an inside piece right sides together with an outside piece. It's important that the two straight edges line up and stay straight.

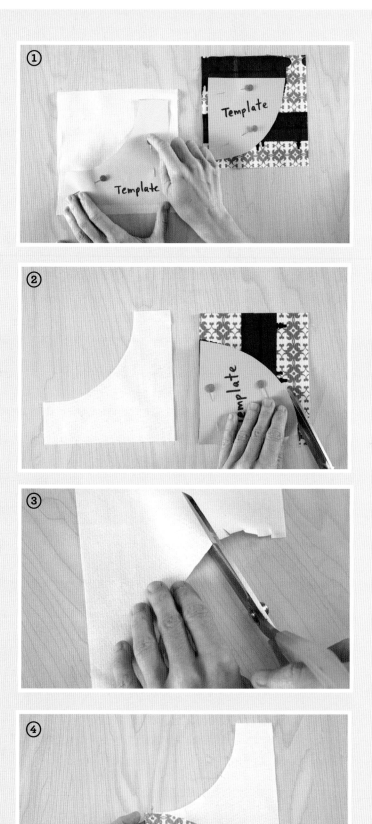

① ② ③ ④

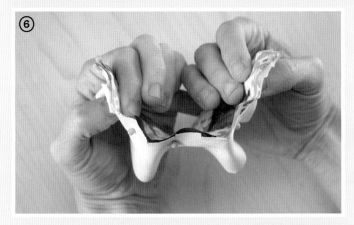

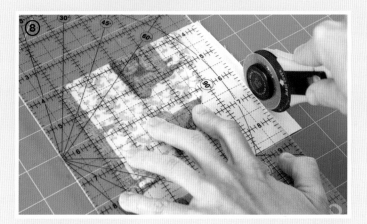

5 Line up the other two straight sides of the curved pieces. It will look peculiar in the middle, but just make sure the edges are lined up straight and pin.

6 Stretch the curve of the white inside piece so the curve fits along the curve of the outside piece. Starting on the left side, line up the edges, making sure there are no puckers, and insert a pin. Go to the opposite side and do the same thing. Keep stretching the inside piece and pinning, moving toward the center, until you have pinned the whole curve.

7 Place the pinned unit under the presser foot. Leave the pins in so the edges remain matched up. It is important to keep the fabrics in alignment. Sew very slowly, checking to make sure that any puckers are flattened out.

8 Remove the fabric from your machine and remove the pins. Press the seam allowance toward the white fabric and trim if necesary.

1 Using the Inside and Outside Curves Templates for Chrissie's block found on page 135, cut nine inside curves from the white material and nine outside curves from a variety of coordinating prints.

2 Using the instructions for *Piecing Curves* on pages 96–97, sew an inside curve to an outside curve.

3 Carefully press your seam allowance toward the white fabric.

4 Repeat steps 2–3 until you have nine curved blocks. Trim each to measure 4³/₈" square.

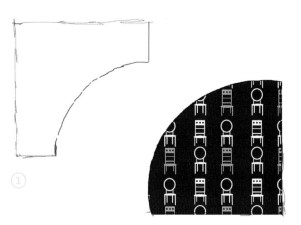

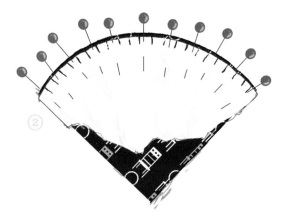

5 Lay out the nine blocks; I oriented all the blocks with the curved portion in the same corner, but try rotating them to create fun and unique designs. Using a standard $\frac{1}{4}$" seam, sew three rows of three blocks together. Sew the three rows together and press. Trim the final block to measure 12" square. Press the seams open.

6 Once you have received all of the blocks from your swap group (see pages 101–104 for the other eleven block instructions), lay out all twelve blocks into four rows of three blocks.

7 Cut eight 3" × 12" strips of gray sashing fabric. Sew a sashing strip to the right side of each block in the first two columns of your quilt. Sew the blocks together to create four rows.

8 Cut five 3" × 40" strips of gray sashing fabric. Sew one strip to the top of the top row and one strip to the bottom of the bottom row. Sew a sashing strip in between each row.

9 Sew the rows of the quilt together. Piece two 3" × 61" strips of gray sashing fabric. Sew one strip to each side of the quilt top. Quilt and bind.

Quote From Angela

"I am HUGELY proud of this block. It is one of the most challenging things I've done in quilting from start to end—and I did it!"

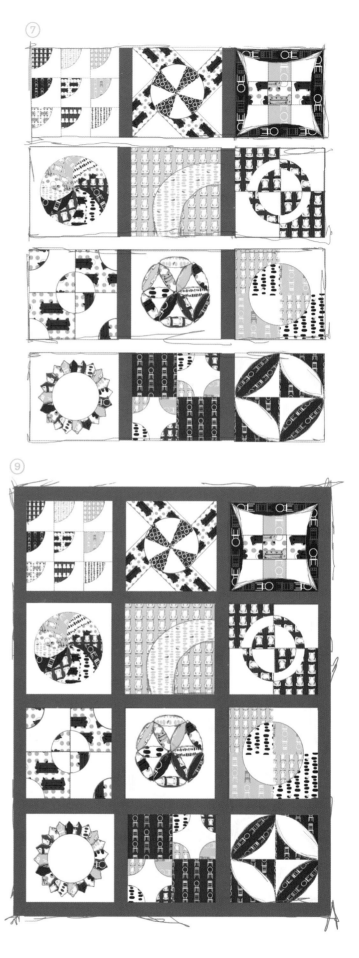

Make the Contributors' Blocks

Note: These instructions are simplified since you now understand the basic method behind sewing curved pieces. Use these instructions to make your quilt, or ask your swappers to make any block with curved piecing or appliqué methods. Use fabric scraps to assemble these blocks, or use the illustrations to guide you when choosing fabrics.

Melanie's Block

Using the template for Melanie's block on page 133, cut two ellipses from the patterned fabric and two from the white fabric. Cut two 6¼" squares from the patterned fabric and two from the white fabric. Using an appliqué method of your choice, stitch each ellipsis diagonally onto a contrasting square as shown. Try to keep the points of the ellipses ¼" away from the block edges. Sew the four quarter blocks together to finish your 12" block.

John's Block

Note: This method yields two 12" blocks.

Place two 14½" squares of printed fabric directly on top of one another. With a rotary cutter (and no ruler), cut out an arc by making two gently curved cuts from the bottom edge of the square to the right edge, cutting through both layers of fabric. Be sure that your cuts are at least ½" away from any corner as well as from each other.

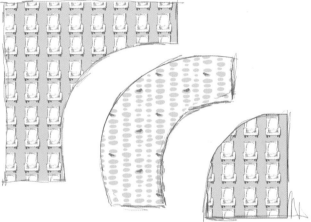

Swap the middle arc from the top block with the arc of the bottom block. Sew the three pieces of each block back together. Use many pins along the curves and sew the seams slowly and carefully to avoid puckers. Trim the blocks down to 12" square.

Angela's Block

Using the three Ring Block Templates for Angela's block on page 134, cut two inside corners, two thin rings and two outside corners from both the patterned and white fabrics. Arrange the pieces in a checkerboard fashion as shown and sew the quarter blocks together. Each small block should measure 6¼"; trim to this size if necessary. Sew the four small blocks together to create your finished 12" block.

Jessica's Block

Using the Swirl Template for Jessica's block on page 135, cut twelve swirls from coordinating prints. Then, cut off the seam allowance from the paper template. Place the template on the wrong side of each wedge and trace along the ouside edge with a pencil—this marks your stitch line. With right sides together, pin the center and end points of two swirl pieces. Add pins in between those points, all the while matching up the drawn-on stitching lines. Carefully sew the swirl pieces together using a small stitch length. Clip the seam allowance of one of the fabrics and press the pieces open. Using an appliqué method of your choice, stitch the finished circular piece to a 12" white background square.

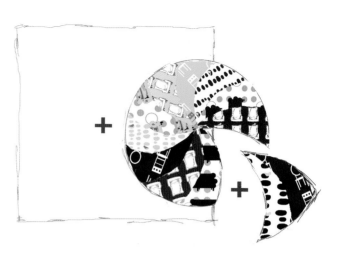

Corey's Block

Using the Petal Template for Corey's block on page 133, trace twelve petal shapes onto double-sided fusible webbing. Cut these shapes out, staying about $1/8$" outside of the traced line. Iron each shape onto the wrong side of coordinating fabric prints. Cut out the petals on the traced line. Place the petals onto a $12^1/_2$" background square and iron them in place, referring to the image for arrangement. Using an appliqué method of your choice, stitch the finished petals onto the background square and trim the block to 12".

Darci's Block

Using the Center and Block Templates for Darci's block on page 134, cut out four curve pieces and four block pieces from the patterned and white fabrics as desired. Mix and match the pieces to form a block with a center circle as shown. Sew each inside curved piece to an outside block piece, clip the seam allowance and press open. This creates four small blocks. Trim each small block to a $6^1/_4$" square. Sew the small blocks together to create your finished 12" block.

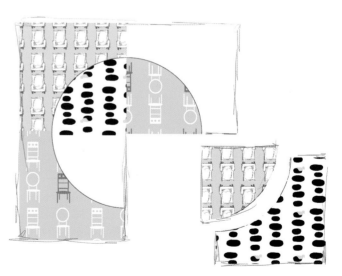

Ryan's Block

From the patterned fabric, cut two 6¼" squares. Using the Curve Template for Ryan's block on page 135, cut eight curved pieces from a variety of patterned fabric. From the white solid fabric, cut two center pieces using the Center Template on page 135. Piece the curved sections into the corners of the center sections. Press and trim both to 6¼" squares. Sew the four blocks together as shown to finish the 12" block.

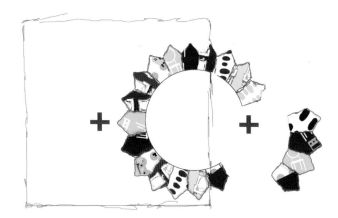

Kerri's Block

For this block, you'll need an Easy Dresden ruler by Wrights. Using the instructions that come with the ruler, cut out twenty 2½" tall plate spokes from your various printed fabrics. Follow the instructions to assemble the spokes to create the Dresden Plate. Appliqué the plate to the center of a 12" square white background block. Use the center circle template provided with the Easy Dresden ruler to cut out a center circle from the white solid fabric. Turn under the edges and appliqué the circle to the center of the Dresden Plate to finish your 12" block.

Beki's Block

From the white fabric, cut four 5" squares. From various patterned prints, cut one 3" square and four 3" × 5" rectangles. Arrange these shapes into a Nine Patch as shown with the small square in the center and the white squares in the corners. Sew the squares together to create a 12" block. Using the template for Beki's block on page 135, cut four curved pieces from a coordinating patterned fabric. Using the appliqué method of your choice, stitch the curved pieces to all sides of the base block.

Note: You only need to stitch down the curved side of the appliqué piece; the other raw edge will be caught in the seam allowance when the block is sewn next to another.

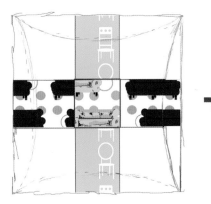

Jennifer's Block

Using the Triangle and Wedge Templates for Jennifer's block on page 134, cut out four triangles from the white fabric, four wedges from the white fabric and four wedges from the patterned fabric. Sew the wedges together to form the interior circle. From the patterned fabric, cut four strips measuring $3^1/_2" \times 10"$. Sew a strip to the right-hand short side of each triangle, and then trim the strips to continue the lines of the triangle, creating four large pieced triangles. Sew the triangles together to create the block base, using the illustration for placement. Using the appliqué method of your choice, stitch the circle to the center of the block. Trim the block to 12" square to finish.

Allison's Block

Note: This method yields two 12" blocks.

Cut two 13" squares, each from a contrasing fabric, and two 6" squares, each from a contrasting fabric (four squares total). Iron double-sided fusible webbing to the wrong side of both 6" squares. Draw or trace a circle onto the wrong side of both 6" squares. Cut out both circles. Remove the fusible web paper from the back of each circle and fuse each circle to the center of the opposite-colored 13" square. Sew around the edges of the circles. Cut each block in half two times. You will end up with eight square pieces (enough for two blocks). Rearrange the pieces in a checkerboard, with a circle in the center as shown, and sew them together. To add circle quarter pieces to the corner of the blocks, cut out another circle from a 6" square and iron fusible webbing to the wrong side. Cut the circle into quarters, fuse and appliqué the pieces into the block corners. Trim the block to 12" square to finish.

Swappers: Chrissie, Jennifer, Beki,
Jessica, John, Angela,
Allison, Corey, Darci,
Kerri, Ryan, Melanie

Quilted by: Mary Beth Krapil

Chapter Four

Gorgeous Gigantic Swaps

In this last chapter, we conquer swaps that can accommodate a large group. One of the first swaps I ever participated in was a Nine Patch Block Swap involving 100 people!

Let's pretend for a second that you are the swap leader of a block swap for 100 people. The first thing you need to do is decide on a relatively easy block and a color scheme. Once you have 100 people signed up, you need to clarify the rules and deadlines. Make sure that everyone has the specifics on the block and color scheme. Be very clear and firm about deadlines, but also take into account that a few people will probably send their blocks a little late. Don't forget to have everyone send either a check or postage stamps to cover shipping the blocks. Then be prepared to receive 100 packages, each containing 100 blocks! Yes, that is 10,000 blocks to sort and resend!

Being a swap leader like this can be stressful if you haven't taken the time to make sure all the details are organized, but if you are prepared and have set clear rules for the swappers, it can be a really fun experience.

If you participate in a very large swap like this one, it is nice to include a small gift for your swap leader for all of his or her hard work, like a nice fat quarter, a $5 gift card to a coffee shop or a small handmade item.

The Invisible Nine Patch Swap

A couple of years ago I participated in my first-ever quilt swap—a Disappearing Nine Patch Swap. The color theme was red and aqua, and 100 people were involved. I remember the feeling of giddiness after receiving my final package in the mail. There were so many variations of fabric, and as I pieced the quilt together, I watched it metamorphose into a real-life kaleidoscope. After collecting fabrics in the popular combination of yellow and gray this past year, I knew that I was ready to host my own Nine Patch swap.

To Lead This Swap, You'll Need:

MATERIALS
- Variety of yellow and gray fabrics
- White thread
- $^3/_4$ yd. of white fabric for border
- 50" × 56" piece of cotton batting
- 50" × 56" piece of fabric for backing
- Dark gray fabric for binding

TOOLS
- Rotary cutter
- Rotary cutting mat
- Acrylic ruler
- Iron
- Scissors
- Pins
- $^1/_4$" foot for piecing
- Free motion foot for quilting

OTHER
- 8 swappers, plus you
- Envelopes
- Postage

How the Swap Works

You need eight swappers plus yourself to make a total of seventy-two blocks. Everyone keeps eight of their own blocks and sends the rest of their blocks to the swap leader. The swap leader will sort and send the blocks so that each swapper receives eight blocks from each participant. Keep in mind that this type of swap can be increased to accommodate a large number of swappers.

Send each swapper their Swap Kit (see below). When I received my blocks, I spent a lot of time playing with patterns until I was pleased with the arrangement. After piecing the blocks together in nine rows of eight blocks each using a standard $^1/_4$" seam, Tasha offered to quilt it. She thought that adding a white border all the way around would help frame out the blocks, and I agreed.

Remember to share your finished quilts in person or through an online photo-sharing Website so everyone can see the final results.

Invisible Nine Patch Swap Kit

- The total number of blocks to make
- Swap instructions
- Block instructions and finished block size
- Information on the colorway and theme for the swap
- Your (Swap Leader's) return address
- Due date

Block Size: 5½" x 5½"
Finished Quilt Size: 46" x 52"

Lining Up Seams Technique

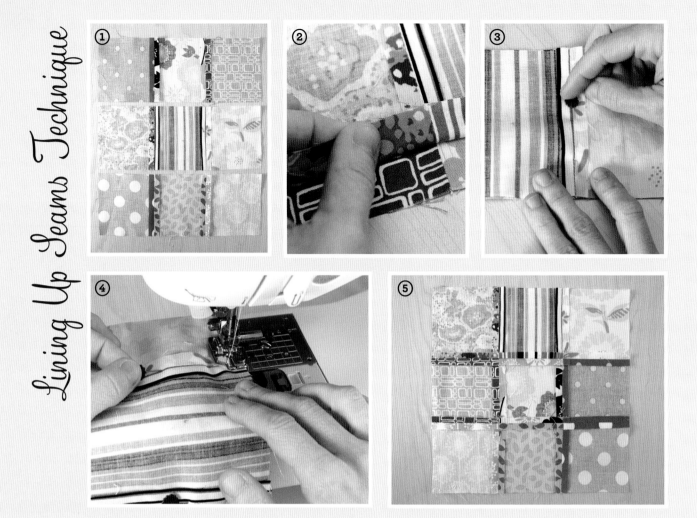

1 When you are ready to join pieces, you always want your seams to line up as accurately as possible. One of the reasons I press my seams open is because I think it's easier to match up the seams this way.

2 When matching seams that have been pressed open, align them on top of each other, right sides together.

3 Put a pin through the center of the seam in both the top and bottom pieces to align.

4 Sew the pieces together carefully, removing the pin at the last second before it reaches your needle.

5 Press the seams open. Your seams should be perfectly aligned if you take the time and care to pin them before sewing.

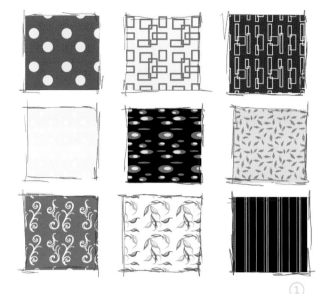

①

②

1 From nine different yellow and/or gray fabrics, cut nine 4" squares. Arrange them in a grid of three rows of three squares. I placed the darker fabrics in the corners and center, creating an X pattern, as shown.

2 Using a standard ¼" seam, sew the top, middle and bottom rows of squares together. Press the seams open.

3 Sew the three rows together, using the technique on page 110 to help you accurately line up all the blocks' seams. Press the seams open. Your block should measure 11" square; trim to this size if necessary.

4 After measuring carefully to determine the true horizontal and vertical center, cut through the middle of the block both ways—top to bottom and side to side. You will end up with four 5½" blocks.

③

④

⑤

5 Once you have made and received all of your blocks, lay them out in nine rows of eight blocks until you are happy with the arrangement. Using a standard $1/4$" seam, sew the blocks together into rows, and then sew the rows together.

6 Add a white border to the outside edges of the quilt. From the white solid fabric, cut two $3^3/_4$" × 41" borders.* Sew these to the top and bottom of the quilt. From the white solid fabric, cut and piece two $3^3/_4$" × 52" borders*. Sew these to the sides of the quilt. Quilt and bind.

Note: For greatest accuracy in adding borders, refer to the instructions on pages 26–27. The lengths given for the borders above are approximate; measure your quilt to determine the best border lengths for your finished quilt.

Layout Variations

When trying to decide your final block arrangement before piecing the quilt top, take some digital photos. Arrange and photograph the blocks laid out in a few different ways. You can then compare the images to see which one you like best.

The Nine Patch block can be varied in many different ways. The Internet is full of free Nine Patch block tutorials for variations such as the Shoo Fly, the Split Nine Patch and Jacob's Ladder.

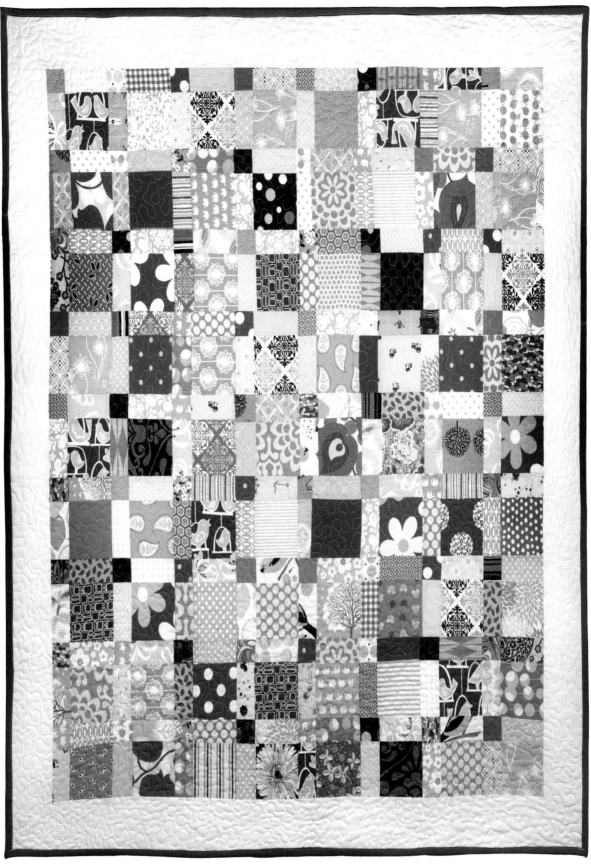

Swappers: Tasha, Nettie, Corey, Angela, Darci, Jennifer, Jessica, Crystal, Chrissie

Assembled by: Chrissie

Quilted by: Tasha

The Vintage Meets Modern Swap

Vintage fabrics have recently made a huge impact in the quilting world. Reminiscent of sleepovers spent at my grandparents' house in the 1970s and 1980s, vintage sheets and pillowcases made their way into my quilting fabric collection. When I saw Allison's brilliant Double Hourglass block tutorial on her blog, I knew I had found the perfect pattern. Vintage fabrics meet a modern pattern! These blocks combined with a white solid fabric make using a large variety of colors and patterns pleasing to the eye.

To Lead This Swap, You'll Need:

MATERIALS
- Sheet of cardstock or template plastic
- Assortment of vintage sheets and pillowcases
- 3 yds. of white solid fabric*
- White thread
- 52" × 67" piece of cotton batting
- 52" × 67" piece of fabric for backing
- Complementary fabric for binding

Kona white used in sample

TOOLS
- Rotary cutter
- Rotary cutting mat
- Acrylic ruler
- Iron
- Scissors
- Pins
- $\frac{1}{4}$" foot for piecing
- Free motion foot for quilting

OTHER
- 9 swappers, plus you
- Envelopes
- Postage

Note: In this instance, prewash all of your fabric. Since vintage sheets and pillowcases have been washed often over the course of their lives, prewash your quilting fabric to keep shrinkage consistent.

How the Swap Works

There are ten swappers total in this swap. Everyone makes their own quilt. The objective is to provide all the other quilters with vintage fabrics that are different from their own.

Everyone makes ninety blocks using their own vintage sheets and pillowcases and a predetermined background fabric (in this case, white solid fabric). Everyone keeps nine of their own blocks and sends the rest of their blocks to the swap leader. The swap leader will sort and send the blocks so that each swapper receives nine blocks from each participant.

Send each swapper their Swap Kit (see below). When I received all of my blocks, I laid them out in a variety of ways until I liked the final placement. I decided on an arrangement of eleven rows of eight blocks each, which left two blocks that I didn't use. I made piles of each row from left to right and labeled the piles. After sewing each row together using a standard $\frac{1}{4}$" seam, I pieced the rows together.

Remember to share your finished quilts in person or through an online photo-sharing Website so everyone can see the final results.

Vintage Meets Modern Swap Kit

- The total number of blocks to make
- Swap instructions
- Block instructions and finished block size
- Information on the colorway and theme for the swap
- Your (Swap Leader's) return address
- Due date

Block Size: 6½" × 6½"
Finished Quilt Size: 47½" × 63"

Lining Up Multiple Seams Technique

This block is a tricky one when it comes to matching up multiple seams, and lots of quilt blocks require you to piece units where multiple seams come together. Here are a few hints for keeping them all straight.

1 Ironing your seams open will eliminate a lot of bulk. Keeping fabric bulk in your seam allowance to a minimum will help a lot when working with multiple seams.

2 Make sure you have your ¼" foot on your machine. If you need to, use a piece of blue painters tape to mark and extend a ¼" line on the machine bed for more accuracy (see page 13).

3 Use a lot of pins. Pinning your blocks together through the matching seams helps ensure success.

And if it doesn't come out totally perfect? Accept that they don't all have to be completely perfect and just enjoy the process!

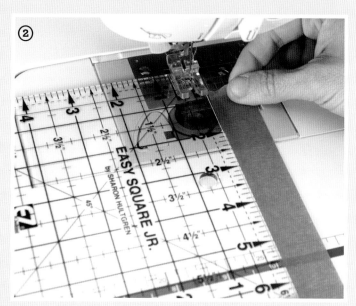

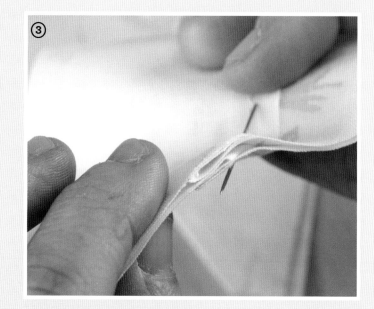

1 From a piece of cardstock or template plastic, cut a $7^{1}/_{2}$" square. Cut again from corner to corner both ways. Use one of the triangles for your template.

2 Cut one $2^{1}/_{4}$" × 42" strip from both the white fabric and the vintage fabric.

3 Using a standard $^{1}/_{4}$" seam, sew the two strips together lengthwise. Press the seam allowance toward the vintage fabric.

4 Place your template on the strip, trying to center it. You may have a little bit of extra fabric on the top and bottom of the triangle. Make a mark on your template along the seam line; use this line to help align all subsequent triangles.

5 Cut the strip along both sides of the template to cut your first triangle. Then turn the template over to match the last cut to the side of the template and cut along the other side.

6 Keep flipping your template and cutting along the left-hand side all the way down the strip set. You will need four triangles to make one block. Each strip set should yield eight triangles for two blocks.

7 Arrange your triangles together to make your block using the illustration as a guide. Sew the triangles together, matching the seams. It's more important for the interior seams to match up than for the exterior edges to match. Press the seam allowances open to reduce bulk.

8 The finished block should measure 6³/₄" square. Trim the block to 6¹/₂" square and press.

9 Once you have made and received all of your blocks, arrange them into eleven rows of eight blocks each. Sew the blocks together into rows, and then sew the rows together to complete the quilt top. Quilt and bind.

Tips on Finding Vintage Fabrics

If you don't have your own collection of vintage sheets or pillowcases, they are easy and fun to find, not to mention inexpensive. I found almost all of mine at thrift stores. I've never paid more than 99 cents for a vintage pillowcase. Once you start collecting them, it becomes a fun challenge to find ones that you don't have.

There are also many eBay and Etsy stores that specialize in vintage fabrics. They sell a nice variety of different pieces. The advantage to buying them online is that it's easy and fast to get a wide variety of pieces.

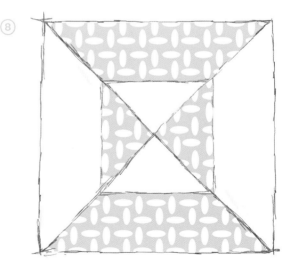

Swappers: Allison, Chrissie, Jessica, Jennifer, Heather, Nettie, Darci, Nova, Beki, Kelly

Assembled by: Chrissie

Quilted by: Jennifer

The Wonky Siggy Swap

I think it would be safe to attribute the wonky block style to modern-day quilters. It is a fun and modern approach to take a traditional quilt block and make it wonky by skewing the placement of the pattern and seams. A siggy (or signature) swap is a traditional quilter's movement that has never gone out of style. Having a siggy swap with the quilters you swap with on a regular basis is a great way to commemorate a special time or occasion. I asked everyone who participated in this book to be in this siggy swap.

To Lead This Swap, You'll Need:

MATERIALS

- Variety of red, pink and aqua fabrics (divided up 18 ways)
- Additional red, pink and aqua scraps for border; each piece must be at least 5½" long
- 3 yds. of white solid fabric cut into 4½" squares*
- White thread
- 50" × 77" piece of cotton batting
- 50" × 77" piece of fabric for backing
- Complementary fabric for binding

Kona white used in sample

TOOLS

- Rotary cutter
- Rotary cutting mat
- Acrylic ruler
- Iron
- Scissors
- ¼" foot for piecing
- Walking foot for quilting
- Fine-tipped permanent fabric marker

OTHER

- 17 swappers, plus you
- Envelopes
- Postage

How the Swap Works

For this particular swap, all participating members design their own siggy swap quilt. You can easily alter these directions to fit the number of people who will be participating in your swap.

Send each swapper their Swap Kit (see below). Ask them to make a block using the instructions and the background fabric provided and to return the block to you on a specified date. My swappers each used the same white background fabric, but their own aqua, pink and red fabrics for the star points.

After receiving my blocks back from the swappers, I stitched them together in six rows of three blocks using a standard ¼" seam. The quilt turned out much longer than it was wide, so I decided to create wide side borders to balance out the design. To complement the wonky stars, I decided to use wonky stripping for the side pieces (see page 122).

Take turns like this until all members of your swap group have had a chance to design their own special siggy quilt.

Remember to share your finished quilts in person or through an online photo-sharing Website so everyone can see the final results.

Wonky Siggy Swap Kit

- (9) 4½" squares of white fabric
- Block instructions
- Instructions on color scheme
- Your return address
- Due date
- **Optional:** Fine-tipped permanent fabric marker for signing (most swappers will have one already)

Block Size: 12½" x 12½"
Finished Quilt Size: 45½" x 72½"

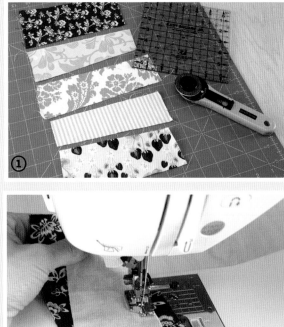

1 Go through your scraps and pick out a variety of fabrics in your color theme. Cut the pieces in a variety of widths, varying from $1^1/_2$" to $3^1/_2$". The length of each strip should be at least $5^1/_2$".

2 Start with two strips. Place them right sides together. Instead of lining the edges up, take the top piece and lay it slightly askew.

3 Using a standard $^1/_4$" seam and keeping your seam allowance even with the edge of the top piece, sew the two pieces together lengthwise.

4 Cut the excess fabric $^1/_4$" away from the seam.

5 Press the pieces open. Continue adding strips in this way, slightly altering the top fabric to the right or left so the strips are wonky.

6 When you have completed piecing all the strips together, press the wonky strip flat. Trim both sides so they are even. You will probably need to take approximately $^1/_4$" off of each side to even up both sides.

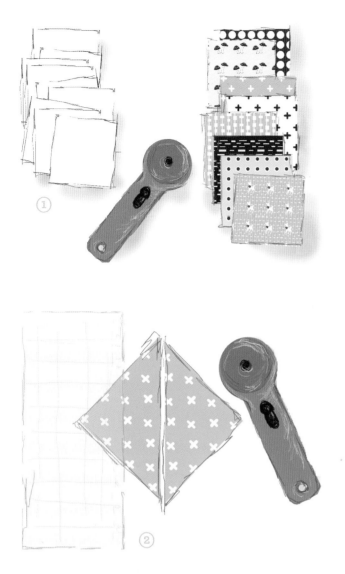

1 From the white fabric, cut nine $4\frac{1}{2}$" squares (background and center). From the colorful prints, cut eight $4\frac{1}{2}$" squares (star points).

2 Cut each colorful square in half diagonally. You will now have sixteen triangles. Set eight aside for another project—you will only need eight of them to make one block.

3 Place four triangles on top of four white squares, right sides together. The triangles should overlap the bottom right corner of each square as shown. If you change the angle of the triangles, you will vary the wonkiness of the star. Stitch along the bottom edge of each tringle.

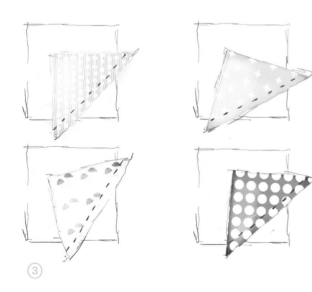

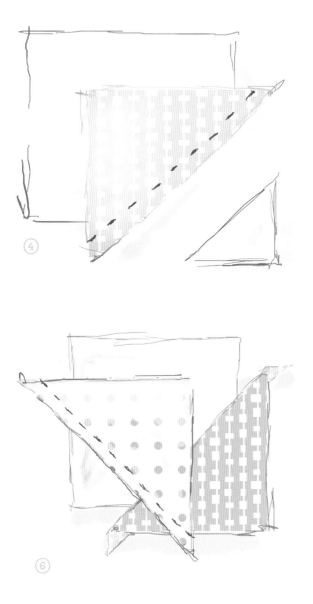

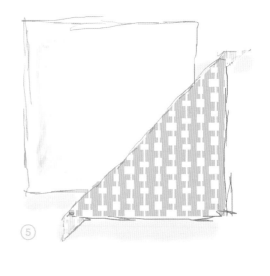

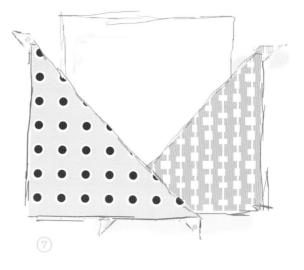

4 Cut the excess fabric ¼" away from the seam.

5 Open up the triangle and press. Repeat this process with the other three squares.

6 Sew the remaining four triangles to the left side of these four background blocks. To vary the wonkiness, leave a space or overlap the triangles at the bottom.

7 Cut off the excess seam allowance on the left side and press the triangles open.

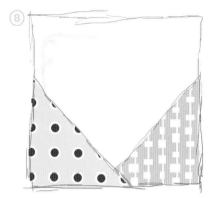

8 Trim each small block to 4½"square.

9 Using a ¼" seam allowance, stitch a completed star point square to both the left and right sides of a solid white square as shown. This will be your middle row.

10 Using a ¼" seam allowance, sew a plain background square to the left and right sides of both remaining star point squares. Use the illustration as a guide.

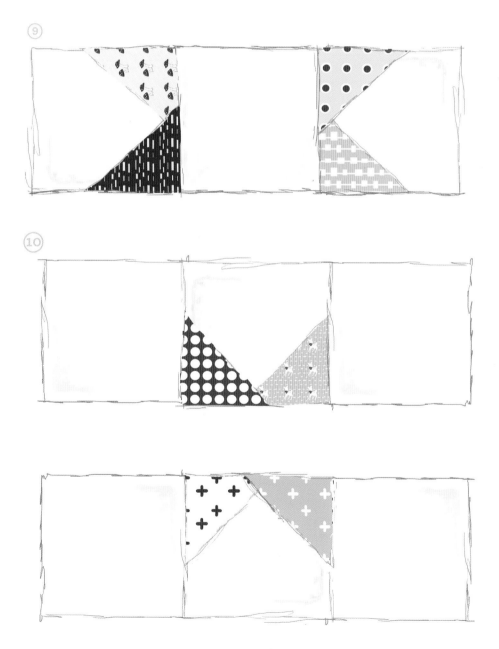

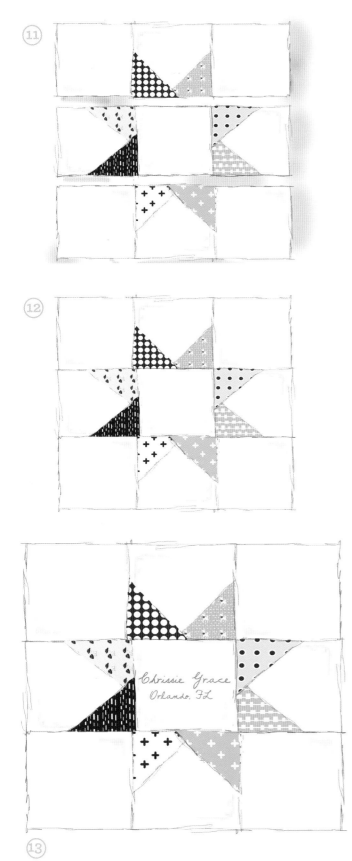

11 Press and iron all three rows. Line up the seams, pin, and stitch the top row to the middle row.

12 Repeat to attach the bottom row. Press again. Your finished block should measure 12$\frac{1}{2}$" square.

13 Using a fine-tipped permanent fabric marker, sign the center square of your block.

14 Once you have received the rest of your siggy blocks, sew them together in six rows of three blocks each.

15 Using the *Wonky Stripping Technique* on page 122 and your red/pink/aqua border scraps (each at least 5$\frac{1}{2}$" long), piece two wonky side borders. Each side border should measure 72$\frac{1}{2}$" long and approximately 5" wide after trimming. Sew a side border to each side of the quilt. Quilt and bind.

The Great Marker Debate

When I sent out the Wonky Siggy Swap instructions to the quilters in my group, there was an immediate response regarding which kind of marker should be used for signing the blocks. The debate was between using an ultra-fine point permanent marker or a permanent fabric marker. Some people voiced a concern over the ultra-fine point permanent marker having the potential to bleed through the fabric. Other people thought that the permanent fabric marker was too light and didn't write as clearly as the ultra-fine point permanent marker.

We ended up deciding that people could choose which marker they wanted to use, and all in all, the results were nearly identical.

Swappers: John, Crystal, Darci, Nova, Corey, Beki, Melanie, Jennifer, Chrissie, Angela, Kelly, Heather, Jessica, Kerri, Allison, Tasha, Nettie, Ryan

Quilted by: Chrissie

Contributor Gallery

Hexagon Pillow
by Corey Yoder

Colorblocks Pillow
by Melanie Sullivan

Triangle Mini Quilt
by Ryan Walsh

Small Coin Quilt
by Ryan Walsh

Christmas Embroidery Quilt
by Corey Yoder

Mushroom Doll Quilt
by Darci Yaden

Double Hourglass Quilt
by Nettie Peterson

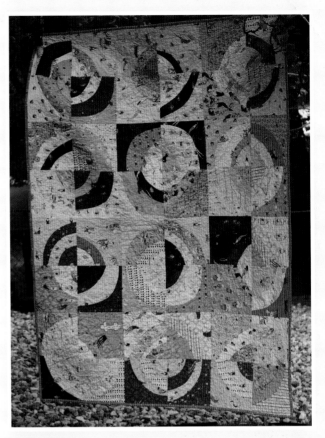

Curved Quilt
by Nettie Peterson

Vintage Wonky Nine Patch Quilt
by Jessica Kovach

Invisible Nine Patch Variation Quilt
by Allison Harris

Patterns and Templates

ALL TEMPLATES ARE DRAWN TO INCLUDE ¹/₄" SEAM ALLOWANCE. PLEASE ENLARGE THE PATTERN OR TEMPLATE AT THE INDICATED PERCENTAGE BEFORE USING.

MY FAVORITE THINGS SWAP

Tree Embroidery Pattern

Shown at 40%; enlarge first at 200%, then enlarge again at 125%

MY FAVORITE THINGS SWAP

Bunny Embroidery Pattern

Shown at 40%; enlarge first at 200%, then enlarge again at 125%

MY FAVORITE THINGS SWAP

Owl Embroidery Pattern

Shown at 40%; enlarge first at 200%, then enlarge again at 125%

MY FAVORITE THINGS SWAP

Cupcakes Embroidery Pattern

Shown at 40%; enlarge first at 200%, then enlarge again at 125%

MY FAVORITE THINGS SWAP

Mushroom House Embroidery Pattern

Shown at 40%; enlarge first at 200%, then enlarge again at 125%

MY FAVORITE THINGS SWAP

Nesting Dolls Embroidery Pattern

Shown at 40%; enlarge first at 200%, then enlarge again at 125%

MY FAVORITE THINGS SWAP

Sewing Machine Embroidery Pattern

Shown at 40%; enlarge first at 200%, then enlarge again at 125%

MY FAVORITE THINGS SWAP

Camera Embroidery Pattern

Shown at 40%; enlarge first at 200%, then enlarge again at 125%

MY FAVORITE THINGS SWAP
Bird Banner Embroidery Pattern
Shown at 40%; enlarge first at 200%, then enlarge again at 125%

FLIGHT OF THE BUMBLEBEE DOLL QUILT
Bee Template
Shown at 100%

6

5

4

3

2

1

THE HEXIE TABLE RUNNER SWAP
Hexagon Template
Shown at 100%

ARGYLE ZIG PILLOW
Pattern A Block
Shown at 100%

THE CURVY BLOCK SWAP
Corey Petal Template
Shown at 100%

THE CURVY BLOCK SWAP
Melanie Template
Shown at 50%; enlarge at 200%

6

5

4

3

2

1

ARGYLE ZIG PILLOW
Pattern B Block
Shown at 100%

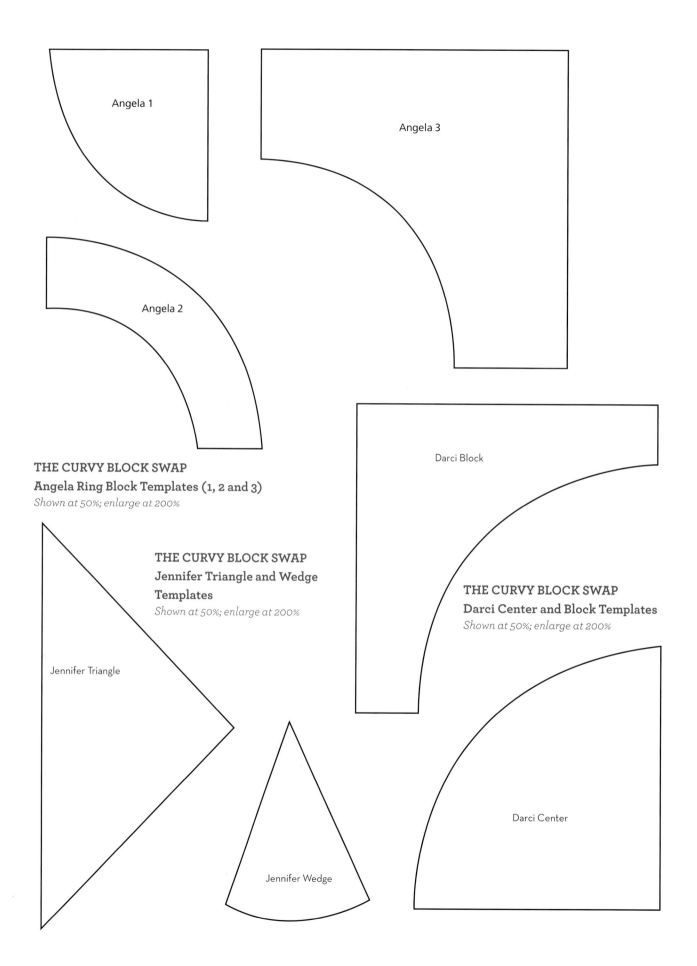

Angela 1

Angela 3

Angela 2

THE CURVY BLOCK SWAP
Angela Ring Block Templates (1, 2 and 3)
Shown at 50%; enlarge at 200%

Darci Block

THE CURVY BLOCK SWAP
Jennifer Triangle and Wedge
Templates
Shown at 50%; enlarge at 200%

THE CURVY BLOCK SWAP
Darci Center and Block Templates
Shown at 50%; enlarge at 200%

Jennifer Triangle

Jennifer Wedge

Darci Center

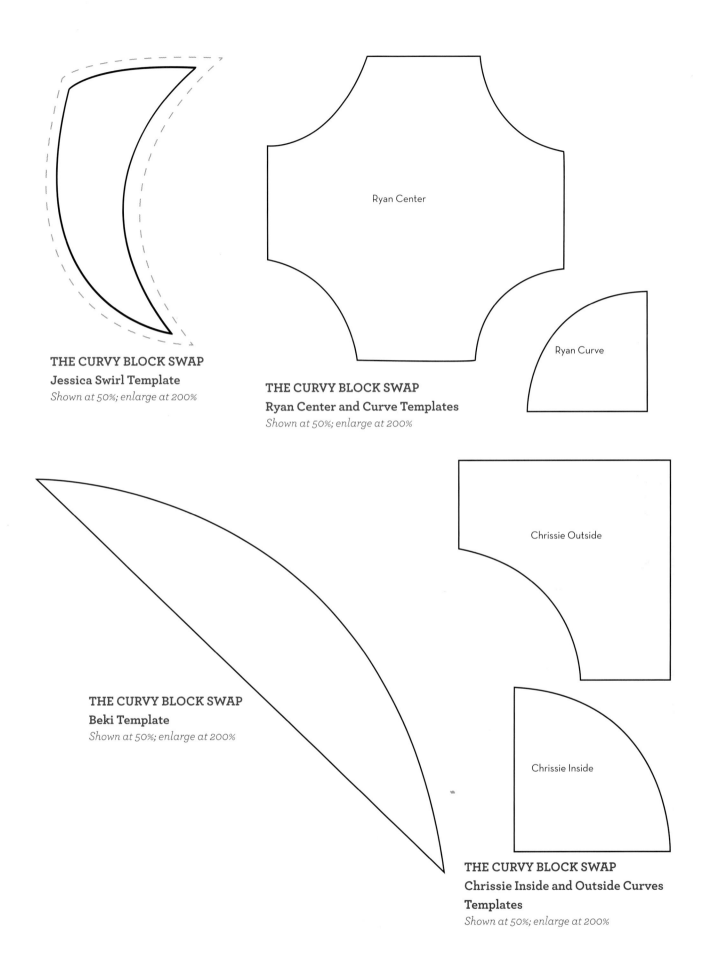

THE CURVY BLOCK SWAP
Jessica Swirl Template
Shown at 50%; enlarge at 200%

THE CURVY BLOCK SWAP
Ryan Center and Curve Templates
Shown at 50%; enlarge at 200%

Ryan Center

Ryan Curve

Chrissie Outside

Chrissie Inside

THE CURVY BLOCK SWAP
Beki Template
Shown at 50%; enlarge at 200%

THE CURVY BLOCK SWAP
Chrissie Inside and Outside Curves Templates
Shown at 50%; enlarge at 200%

About the Author

CHRISSIE GRACE
is the author of three other books published by North Light Books: *Wild Tiles*, *Tiles Gone Wild* and *Sharing Stitches*. She cannot commit to just one type of art—she loves mixed media, mosaics, quilting and sewing, photography, painting and collage. Chrissie's work focuses on the whimsical and colorful aspects of life, and shows the expansion of her creativity.

In addition to being a full-time artist, Chrissie is also a full-time mom and wife. She lives and works just outside of Orlando, Florida, with her precious family. For daily inspiration and to see more of Chrissie's work, check out her blog at www.chrissiegrace.blogspot.com. You can purchase her one-of-a-kind items at www.mixedmediamama.etsy.com.

About the Illustrator

ARIEL ELDRIDGE
spends her days corralling her two little sweetcake boys and plays the role of illustrator by night. She received her BA in art education from Purdue University and has used it to teach in public schools as well as a variety of other forums. Published in the 2011 Sewing Calendar by Accord Publishing, Ariel is also a self-taught quilter. Her love of color and fabric has propelled her into the world of fabric design. You can find her Pocketful of Pinwheels illustrated fabric designs both on Spoonflower.com and Etsy.com. Catch Ariel in the creative process on her blog, www.arieleldridge.blogspot.com.

ALLISON HARRIS fell in love with quilting four years ago after her first son was born. Since then, quilting has blessed her life and become a true passion. She writes a quilting, sewing and life blog called Cluck. Cluck. Sew., and recently started a small quilt-pattern business. She loves teaching anyone to quilt and hopes that quilting will continue to be popular with younger generations. Allison currently resides in Idaho and works as a full-time mother, a part-time dental hygienist, and a naptime quilter. Her ultimate goal is to open sewing school programs in impoverished nations that will improve and sustain the lives of women. Allison can be found blogging at www.cluckclucksew.com.

ANGELA NASH is a stay-at-home mom who loves to quilt. She used library books, the Internet, and trial and error to teach herself how to quilt. She has been crafty all her life, always making one thing or another. Angela was a mechanical engineer before having kids, so she is very math-oriented with her quilting and enjoys getting out graph paper and a calculator when planning her next project. As an engineer, she's all about the process and tends toward neatness and perfection—her goal is always to try to fit some kind of actual creativity into that mix! That's where swaps and quilting bees really help push her quilting. Quilting has been the perfect hobby to join together her love of making things, math, and giving handmade gifts to people. Angela and her family live in a Chicago suburb. You can follow Angela's blog at mythreesonsknit.blogspot.com.

BEKI LAMBERT lives with her husband and three children on the outskirts of Baton Rouge, Louisiana. She inherited her love of sewing from her mother and grandmother. She enjoys creating bags, purses, quilts and her own sewing-pattern line. Although she put crafting on hold during her first years as a mother, Beki is back at it, thanks in part to the discovery of craft blogs. The daily feedback and sharing of ideas through blogging keeps her inspired. Beki has contributed to Lark Books' Pretty Little series, the Craft Hope book, and Interweave Press' *Stitch* magazine. Visit her online at www.artsycraftybabe.typepad.com and www.artsycraftybabe.etsy.com.

COREY YODER is a fabric-loving, full-time mom with a passion for all things quilty and fabric-related. As a fourth-generation quilter, Corey has been surrounded by fabric and quilts her whole life. However, it was not until after her marriage in 1997 that her passion for fabric and quilts really began. Corey's love of fabric led her to quilt-making, followed by the opening of her children's clothing and appliqué business, Little Miss Shabby, and finally, full circle back to quilts and quilt design. Corey's work focuses on traditional quilts and quilt blocks with a modern flair. Her designs often combine a mix of tradition, embroidery and appliqué, utilizing bright and fun fabrics. Corey lives and works in a quaint Amish town in Ohio with her husband and two daughters. To see more of Corey's work and design process, visit her blog at www.littlemissshabby.blogspot.com.

CRYSTAL JOHNSEN is a stay-at-home mother to two. She spends her time creating in some form or another, be it quilting, sewing, baking, photography or making dinner for her two sweet boys and wonderful husband. Her work leans toward the nonconventional side—Crystal does a lot of "bend the rules" sewing, focusing on bright colors and funky combinations. You can catch up with her at www.littlebitfunky.com where she shares about her love of family, sewing and Jesus.

DARCI YADEN'S lifelong love for sewing came from her mother who taught her how to sew when she was just a young girl. Darci loves to make clothes and to quilt, as is evident by her involvement in the online sewing and blogging community, through her blog Stitches and Scissors, and her participation in numerous virtual quilting bees and swaps. Darci and her work have been featured in *Fat Quarterly* e-magazine, and she is a member of the Orange County Modern Quilt Guild. Darci loves to create, and sells her work on Etsy. She lives in Orange County, California, with her husband and two young daughters who are a continual source of inspiration. Visit Darci at www.stitchesandscissors.com.

HEATHER BOSTIC ({House} of A La Mode) is the mother of two beautiful boys, an adoring wife and an autism activist living in beautiful Portland, Oregon. Sewing was an easy choice for relaxation while raising a child with autism, although what started out as a hobby for her has turned into a manic compulsion that has an appetite of its very own. She just can't help herself! Combine that with her Flickr and blog life and you have one serious non-stop party! This is her . . . keeping it real . . . in all her glory! alamodefabric.blogspot.com

JESSICA KOVACH AND JENNIFER FORTUNA are twins who love to create, craft, design and quilt. Their love of crafting goes back generations—their mother and grandmother passed down a love of creating projects with their hands. Both Jessica and Jennifer learned how to sew at an early age just from watching their mother and have taught others how to sew throughout the years. Jessica lives in West Olive, Michigan, with her husband and three children. She enoys designing and experimenting with colors to create new designs in quilting. She is also talented in making clothing, home décor items and designing new appliqué and quilting patterns. Jennifer lives about an hour away from her sister in Rockford, Michigan, with her husband and two children. She was an interior designer before turning stay-at-home mom. She loves creating with fabric, drawing and taking vintage craft ideas and turning them into new decorations for today. To see more of Jennifer and Jessica's work, check out their blog at www.twinfibers.blogspot.com.

JOHN ADAMS is a husband and father of three who enjoys sewing and quilting in his spare time. Inspired by the growing number of crafting blogs and the emergence of vibrant, modern quilting fabrics in the textile industry, John convinced his wife to teach him how to use her sewing machine in 2004 and hasn't looked back. He started his popular blog, QuiltDad.com, in 2008 to share his love of patchwork with others. Since then, John has become very active in the online quilting communities. Today, he applies his modern quilting aesthetic by designing quilt patterns for both fabric designers and companies and contributing frequently to creative blogs, books and other collaborative endeavors. John is also a co-founder of the popular e-magazine *Fat Quarterly*. John and his family live in Cary, North Carolina.

KELLY BISCOPINK made her first quilt with her mom when she was seven years old and hasn't stopped sewing since! A voracious reader, writer and crafter, Kelly is very lucky to edit and help create the craft books she loves to drool over in bookstores. She is a proud member of the Cincinnati Modern Quilt Guild and the writer of a quilting blog that tends toward the quirky side of life. Visit Kelly at stitchyquiltstuff.blogspot.com.

KERRI HORSLEY is a mother to six sweet children, a wife to a loving husband and a crafter and blogger who lives in the Seattle, Washington, area. She is a former Montessori teacher who tries to incorporate its teachings into her home. As a result of being born in Tehran, Iran, and spending a couple years in Shanghai, China, Kerri loves to travel. Her spring and summer days are often spent taking day trips to the beach and parks with her family. Kerri also runs a small business, Sew Deerly Loved, with the help of her devoted husband. You can find her at www.sewdeerlyloved.etsy.com and their soon-to-come Website www.sewdeerlyloved.com. Be sure to stop by her blog and say hi at www.lovelylittlehandmades.blogspot.com.

MELANIE SULLIVAN began sewing as a child and grew up with a passion to create. After receiving a degree in fashion design and art, Melanie's career has focused on retail merchandising and home textile design, but she has never abandoned her love of creating. In addition to sewing, Melanie keeps her hands busy metalworking, lampworking, creating jewelry, knitting and crocheting, and on occasion, painting. Melanie only recently discovered the world of quilting and has embraced being a part of the online community of creative bloggers around the world. She enjoys working with bright colors and bold patterns and has developed a love for hand quilting. Melanie's textile design background has found new life in the quilting world, and she hopes to spend more time in the future focused on quilting textiles. Melanie lives in Fort Worth, Texas, with her supportive husband and creative daughter. To see what Melanie is currently working on, visit her blog at www.texasfreckles.com.

NETTIE PETERSON lives in Denver, Colorado, with her husband and three children, and finds time to quilt during naptime and after bedtime. Other than quilting, she enjoys photography, gardening, bike rides, the outdoors, thunderstorms and being with her family. Nettie blogs at aquiltisnice.blogspot.com. Visit her shop, nettiepete.etsy.com.

NOVA FLITTER has always been a little bit crafty, cutting and gluing and sewing and sticking for as long as she can remember. Her real passion for quilting was sparked about ten years ago after emigrating to Australia and buying her very own sewing machine. With a sewing machine in the house 24/7, Nova just wanted to sew, sew, sew! In addition to quilts, she also loves making small projects like pillows, bags, home goods and clothing. She'll often be found in her pajamas with a cuppa' by her side and needle and thread in hand. Nova's eclectic style and taste see her flitting from the simple to the whimsical, the traditional-with-a-modern-twist to slow-cooked hand stiches, from muted tones to a rainbow spectrum and beyond. You can see what Nova's been up to on her blog, www.acuppaandacatchup.com, and over at www.fatquarterly.com.

RYAN WALSH is a self-taught quilter and quilt designer who enjoys taking vintage quilt designs and updating them with a modern twist. He's employed full time as a New York State licensed funeral director and manages a funeral establishment in his hometown. A busy dad, he finds time for his quilting adventures in the late hours after his kids are in bed. Ryan uses quilting to satisfy his never-ending need to be creative. His work is based on combining traditional piecing methods with free-style construction techniques. To challenge his ability, Ryan participates in several online bees and quilt-related swaps every year. When he's not quilting, Ryan also enjoys photography, embroidery, collage, crocheting, sightseeing and spending time with his family. Co-owner of the quilt design company Patchwork Squared (www.patchworksquared.com), Ryan currently resides in the Catskill Mountain region of upstate New York with his wife and children. To see more of Ryan's work, visit his blog at www.ryanwalshquilts.com.

TASHA NOEL has had the desire to create since a young age. Drawing, coloring and painting with her sisters, sewing little dolls, and doing arts and crafts with her mother are some cherished memories from childhood. As an adult, Tasha continues to experiment and enjoy many art forms. Whether it's drawing, sewing, quilting, embroidery, decorating her home or learning a new photography trick, her need to create is evident. Currently, Tasha has an Etsy shop called A Little Sweetness, where she sells her whimsical, childlike embroidery patterns, illustrations and other paper products, as well as her own fabric designs. She is married to her husband, Peter, has five children, and lives in the Seattle, Washington area. You can peek into her world of motherhood and design at www.tashahorsley.typepad.com or shop for products at www.etsy.com/shop/alittlesweetness.

Resources

Clover
WWW.CLOVER-USA.COM
SEWING NOTIONS

Flickr
WWW.FLICKR.COM
PHOTOSHARING

Free Spirit
WWW.FREESPIRITFABRIC.COM
*ANNA MARIA HORNER, DENYSE
SCHMIDT AND OTHER FABRICS*

Gingher
WWW.GINGHER.COM
*SCISSORS, SNIPS AND
OTHER NOTIONS*

Moda
WWW.UNITEDNOTIONS.COM
OLIVER + S AND OTHER FABRICS

Modern Quilt Guild
THEMODERNQUILTGUILD.COM
GET CONNECTED LOCALLY!

Munki Munki
WWW.MUNKIMUNKI.COM
PAJAMAS TO BE USED AS FABRIC

Kokka
WWW.KOKKA.CO.JP/EN
HEATHER ROSS AND IMPORT FABRICS

Prym Consumer USA Inc.
WWW.DRITZ.COM
NIMBLE THIMBLE, NOTIONS

Robert Kauffman Fabrics
WWW.ROBERTKAUFMAN.COM
*KONA SOLIDS, LAURIE WISBRUN AND
OTHER FABRICS*

Spoonflower
WWW.SPOONFLOWER.COM
*CREATE YOUR OWN FABRIC AND BUY
ORIGINAL DESIGNS. HEATHER ROSS
FABRICS*

Wrights
WWW.WRIGHTS.COM
EASY DRESDEN TOOL, NOTIONS

Photo courtesy of Angela Nash

Index

 www.fwmedia.com

15 14 13 12 11   5 4 3 2 1

DISTRIBUTED IN CANADA BY FRASER DIRECT
100 Armstrong Avenue
Georgetown, ON, Canada L7G 5S4
Tel: (905) 877-4411

DISTRIBUTED IN THE U.K. AND EUROPE BY F&W MEDIA INTERNATIONAL
Brunel House, Newton Abbot, Devon, TQ12 4PU, England
Tel: (+44) 1626 323200, Fax: (+44) 1626 323319
Email: enquiries@fwmedia.com

DISTRIBUTED IN AUSTRALIA BY CAPRICORN LINK
P.O. Box 704, S. Windsor NSW, 2756 Australia
Tel: (02) 4577-3555

SRN: Y1783
ISBN-10: 1-4402-1590-1
ISBN-13: 978-1-4402-1590-2

Edited by Kelly Biscopink
Designed by Corrie Schaffeld
Production coordinated by Greg Nock
Photographed by Christine Polomsky, Al Parrish and Corrie Schaffeld
Illustrated by Ariel Eldridge

Metric Conversion Chart

To convert	to	multiply by
Inches	Centimeters	2.54
Centimeters	Inches	0.4
Feet	Centimeters	30.5
Centimeters	Feet	0.03
Yards	Meters	0.9
Meters	Yards	1.1

Acknowledgments

Many thanks to Tonia Davenport and F +W Media for choosing me to work with again. I would like to thank Vanessa Lyman for her patience while we navigated through the beginning of the process. To Christine Polomsky who I was lucky enough to work with again—thank you for your hospitality and generosity. I especially want to thank my editor, and now friend, Kelly Biscopink. You kept me organized and made the whole experience a fun one. Thank you for the lunches, the conversations, the inside jokes and all the quilting tips. I'd also like to thank Ariel Eldridge who did an amazing job on the illustrations for our book. Last, I'd like to thank Corrie Schaffeld for designing our book with a beautiful aesthetic that was more than I imagined. Thanks everyone!

Dedication
This book is dedicated to my love, my husband Mike. Mike, you are the yin to my yang, the right to my left, the north to my south. Thank you for always supporting my dreams and encouraging my creative endeavors. Thank you also for keeping me grounded when my artsy side needs a little balancing out. I am so lucky to have you in my life. I love you.

Connect ~ Inspire ~ Create

Join our online craft community for exclusive offers and daily doses of inspiration.

f fwcraft   t @fwcraft

For unique projects, great techniques and fresh ideas, check out our editor's picks:

Sharing Stitches
One-of-A-Kind Projects to Sew and Swap
Chrissie Grace

Join Chrissie Grace and fifteen talented artists as they exchange fabrics, collaborate on quilts and swap plenty of inspiration on the pages of *Sharing Stitches*. Stitch by stitch, Chrissie shows you how to create colorful and eclectic projects as unique as the group that sews them, including a patchwork pullover, a lace-embellished headband, a large-scale collaborative quilt and a round-robin journal. Break out your sewing machine, round up your friends and start sewing!

3-Fabric Quilts
Quick Techniques for Simple Projects
Leni Levenson Wiener

In *3-Fabric Quilts*, Leni Levenson Wiener gives you the tools to make twelve fantastic quilts, each requiring only three fabrics. You'll get helpful advice on choosing the three fabrics, including tips on understanding color, value and print scale. Illustrated instructions for twelve quilts, each with yardage requirements and instructions for a small and large size, make quilting fun, whether you're a beginner or advanced quilter. With a few simple tricks and tips, choose just three fabrics and be on your way to a fabulous finished quilt!